Advance Praise for
What Do White Americans Owe Black People?

"One of the boldest living thinkers, Jason D. Hill, takes a sledgehammer to everything we've been taught about race and race relations. Written with grace and clarity, *What Do White Americans Owe Black People?* offers a compelling, unifying vision that moves us beyond the current racial hysteria. It should be mandatory reading for every single American."

—**Dr. Peter Boghossian**, Author of *How to Have Impossible Conversations*

"In his latest courageous contribution, Jason Hill rebuts the arguments that white Americans owe reparations to African Americans. Enslavement, he argues, was not a peculiar crime perpetrated by 'whites' against 'blacks' but a commonplace outcome when Europeans—and Arabs—encountered sub-Saharan societies where slave labor was the norm. In stark contrast to the tragic fate of the Africans shipped to the New World colonies, the American Founding posited a revolutionary idea of liberty for all men, though it took two more 'foundings'—the Civil War and Civil Rights—to fulfill that promise for the descendants of slaves in the United States. Tragically, Hill argues, the achievement was swiftly undermined by well-intentioned but destructive welfare policies and the race-conscious ideology that produced both Black Power and Black Lives Matter. This is a bold—and at times, startling—intervention in one of the most contentious debates of our time."

—**Niall Ferguson**, Milbank Family Senior Fellow, The Hoover Institution

"Names like Ta-Nehisi Coates, Ibram X. Kendi, and Nikole Hannah-Jones have come to dominate the debate over slavery reparations and social inequality. Jason Hill's new book demonstrates why theirs should not be the final word. *What Do White Americans Owe Black People?* lays out both the philosophical and practical problems with the concept of inherited guilt. Moreover, it uses facts and logic to expose the sloppy arguments that often pass for deep thinking about race in America today."

—**Jason L. Riley**, *Wall Street Journal* columnist and author of
Maverick: A Biography of Thomas Sowell

"In the grand fashion of Thomas Sowell and in keeping with his previous work, *We Have Overcome*, Jason Hill starts from the philosophical premises of identitarian groupthink, details the lethal consequences if one's concern is a free society, and equips the reader with the intellectual weaponry to combat the neo-Marxists' ideology. Jason doesn't just issue the cri de cœur, 'The individual must rise.' He leads by example. Jason's life, the clarity of his thinking, and his moral courage make his work an indispensable part of any serious discussion of race, justice, and liberty in America."

—**Dan Proft**, Radio Host, *Chicago's Morning Answer* (AM 560-WIND)

Also by Jason D. Hill

*We Have Overcome: An Immigrant's
Letter to the American People*

WHAT DO

WHITE AMERICANS
⎯OWE⎯ BLACK

PEOPLE?

RACIAL JUSTICE
IN THE AGE OF POST-OPPRESSION

JASON D. HILL

EMANCIPATION
BOOKS

AN EMPANCIPATION BOOKS BOOK
An Imprint of Post Hill Press
ISBN: 978-1-64293-794-7
ISBN (eBook): 978-1-64293-795-4

What Do White Americans Owe Black People?:
Racial Justice in the Age of Post-Oppression
© 2021 by Jason D. Hill
All Rights Reserved

Cover Design by Tiffani Shea

Post Hill Press
New York • Nashville
posthillpress.com

Published in the United States of America
1 2 3 4 5 6 7 8 9 10

The person who sins is the one who will die. The child will not be punished for the sins of the parents, and the parent will not be punished for the sins of the child. Righteous people will be rewarded for their own righteous behavior, and wicked people will be punished for their own wickedness.

Ezekiel 18:20

To Dr. Bob Shillman
A magnanimous man. A kind and gentle friend.

CONTENTS

INTRODUCTION

A friend of mine told me an apocryphal story that left me with a cold shudder. He is an old-fashioned "liberal" and a strong advocate of public education; all his children attend public schools. In fact, he is vehemently opposed to the idea of promoting private schools on the premise that they result in a more stratified society because, he believes, poor whites and blacks will be disproportionately disqualified from attending such institutions.

In good faith, he has always entrusted his children's education to what I had typically referred to as "government schools." He was confident that they would receive a robust education.

During the Covid-19 pandemic, however, he was forced to monitor their classroom activities. Unemployment had left him more time to inconspicuously *sit-in*, especially on the classes of his sixth grade son.

One afternoon, he was shocked to come upon an assignment being conducted during an English class in which all the white students in the Zoom course were required to place their arms beside a brown paper bag. (How his son had acquired a crisp, brown paper bag was a mystery to him.) The teacher asked them if they noticed a difference in color between their skin and the brown paper bag. All of the white students nodded, and some verbally assented. The teacher then asked if the color of the bag looked close to the color of some of their classmates who identified as black. His son peered at the screen and raised the icon button identifying his acknowledgement. The teacher then announced the following with full moral rectitude and intransigence:

> "If your skin color is different from the color of the paper bag, then you are part of a problem in America known as 'systemic racism' that does irreparable harm to all black and brown people in America. Further, if your skin color is different from the brown paper bag and you identify as white, you enjoy something called 'white privilege,' which means you are practicing racism every day without knowing it."

Each student that had different color skin than the brown paper bag bore a collective guilt. The teacher then went on to ask the class if they had ever heard the term "reparations."

Out of some sense of visceral, atavistic paternal protection, my friend slammed down his son's computer and told him to go to his room for a while. He said he stood with his fingers pressed into the metal cover of the computer, shaking with incredulity.

I explained to him that guilt implied wrongdoing and that—because his son at age twelve had committed no egregious harm against any black person—he would eventually grow to feel a sense of resentment. Over time, as his mind grew more focused and the charges against him had been codified into a cultural norm, he would feel that he was the real cause of all harms directed at black people. I told him that something evil and sinister was going to take root in his son's psyche.

My friend grew alarmed, but I pressed on. His son, I told him, would grow to feel resentment towards black people. It would be mild at first—a contemptuous discharge fueled by a growing sense of his superiority and empowerment that he, by the power of his whiteness, could cause so much harm and that he, by that same magical power of whiteness, could alleviate the misery and suffering of blacks. I told him it would not end well, and his son's curriculum would continue to include a phalanx of black and white progressive nihilists who would call for the annihilation of "whiteness," which his mind would come to understand as the annihilation of all white people, including himself.

His son, I told him, runs the risk of not only becoming a racist, but a white supremacist. He will come to believe that becoming a white supremacist will be his only default position from which to protect his life from the assault being waged against it—starting with the seemingly benign comparison between his skin color and that of a brown paper bag. And all this would come from white liberals masquerading as anti-racists.

Be careful how you proceed with his education, I warned him. It is not too late for you to assume responsibility and assert control of his mind by extracting him from one of the many national security threats destroying American civilization—our government schools on the tertiary level and our nation's universities. The decision was his.

This book is written against the backdrop of continuous proclamations that white Americans are morally and financially indebted to black people in the United States of America.

In February 2020, Governor Gavin Newsom led California to become the first state in the country to study and develop proposals for potential reparations. As he affixed his signature to these proposals, he responded to what the demanders for reparations were saying: "I like the spirit of what you guys are saying... this is not just about California. This is about making an impact, a dent across the rest of the country."

Apparently, what Newsom liked hearing was implacable assertions of Assemblywoman Shirley Weber, who authored the legislation. She declared boldly:

> "Even though those who lived under slavery are not the actual slave holders, they benefited from the resources of their forefathers, they benefited from racism, they benefited from having white privilege in this country. And the wealth that they have amassed was on the backs, on the discrimination on the backs of African Americans.
>
> "This country has never really felt it owed African Americans anything as a result of slavery."

District Supervisor Shamann Walton introduced legislation to shepherd reparations in San Francisco. Walton was able to redirect $120 million from the San Francisco Police Department to the black community; this was made possible through discussions with the city's mayor and community leaders.

Asheville, North Carolina also unanimously approved a reparations resolution for black residents.

The reparations legislation known as H.R. 40, which has the support of President Biden and the endorsement of Vice President Harris, establishes the Commission to Study and Develop Reparation Proposals for African Americans. It was introduced in the United States House of Representatives on January 4, 2021. The commission shall examine slavery and discrimination in the colonies and the United States from 1619 to the present and recommend appropriate remedies. The commission shall identify (1) the role of the federal and state governments in supporting the institution of slavery, (2) forms of discrimination in the public and private sectors against freed slaves and their descendants, and (3) lingering negative effects of slavery on living African Americans and society.

In writing about the need for reparations, black writer and entertainer Ta-Nehisi Coates documents acts of racial discrimination against blacks after the passage of the 1964 Civil Rights Act, which granted them full legal standing before the law. These discriminatory acts, however, belonged in courts of law. Coates observes that in the 1960s and early 1970s, many blacks, operating under the auspices of various protectionist organizations, were not appealing to government simply for equality. They were no longer fleeing their racially-biased neighborhoods in hopes of better lives elsewhere. *They were charging society with a crime against their community,* and they wanted it ruled as such. In 1968, those aggrieved were no longer seeking the protection of the law. They were seeking reparations.

Coates's pleas for reparations are based on, on among other things, an understanding that black job applicants without a criminal record enjoy roughly the same chance of getting hired as a white applicant with a criminal record.

This is such an egregious lie that the only reason not to ignore it is that the most hyperbolic and lugubrious writer I have ever read in the last thirty-five years has moral credibility not only among blacks but also among well-intentioned whites who have become slaves to his anti-American rhetoric. For some twisted, sadomasochistic reason, they allow themselves to be bullied by writers like Coates into making them feel they are morally and financially responsible for black suffering.

According to Coates, reparations would close the wealth gap since it illustrates the enduring legacy of our country's shameful history of treating black people as sub-citizens, sub-Americans, and sub-humans. In my view—since the alleged "shameful wealth gap" is not irreducibly, causally linked to racial discrimination, as it equally applies to poverty-stricken white persons living below the nationally accepted metric of what defines poverty, and, further, since very poor whites have also been locked out of credit and loan programs shepherding them towards home ownership—society, including wealthy and middle-class blacks, would owe such groups reparations.

Black nationalists who espouse black nationalism (the virtues of which Coates extols while condemning white nationalism) always declare that white supremacy is not merely the work of hotheaded demagogues or a matter of false consciousness but, rather, so fundamental to America that it is difficult to imagine the country without it.

There are two salient points to be made here. According to alt-leftists, the discrimination against poor whites in the housing market cannot be a contender because white skin cancels out any semblance of a legitimate claim to victimhood, and the poorest white can still be a white supremacist. Those vices disqualify them from a moral hearing for their discriminatory grievances.

The new racial narcissists and the narcissism exposed in this book highlight the entire edifice on which the reparation arguments are made and the absence of a morally coherent foundation to uphold them. Reparations for blacks, I show in the ensuing chapters, have been in the making since not just since the Emancipation Proclamation but since 1776 and the creation of the United States Constitution.

But the reparations claims must retreat even farther. If whites as a racial group (many of whose ancestors did not own slaves or whose ancestors arrived after the Civil War) are morally and financially indebted to blacks because of the former's racial identity, then white Americans are forever damned as *individuals* who happen to be white. As we shall see, spurred by the moral framework of Coates and the alt-left, the only solution for these persons is to "abolish whiteness." We will come to see that this catchphrase is a really a call for white extinction.

Among other things, this book picks up where my previous book, *We Have Overcome: An Immigrant's Letter to the American People*, left off. What are the roots of that philosophy of collective racial blame, and how do we combat it?

If whites are to blame for the socioeconomic privations that still exist today among blacks as a result of the residual effects of slavery (a dubious claim I analyze carefully), then how did the slave become a slave? I don't just mean in the literal sense of being taken captive by European traders. I mean: How did the African indigene actually turn him or herself into a slave in the first place? How did he become such easy prey for the European colonizer? There are two factors to consider.

The first elucidating point of clarification is that moral culpability for slavery is complex. As even the chair of the African-American Studies Department at Harvard, Henry Louis Gates, stated in a *New York Times* op-ed in 2010:

> "[...]90 percent of those shipped to the New World enslaved by Africans and then sold to European traders. The sad truth is that

> without the complex business partnerships be-
> tween African elites and European commercial
> traders and commercial agents, the slave trade to
> the New World would have been impossible, at
> least on the scale it occurred."

The truth is that Africans were exchanged in a lengthy process of slave trading whereby they kidnapped and sold each
other long before the Europeans arrived on the shores of Africa.
Slavery existed in Africa among Africans, as will be made clear
in the course of this book. By the time the Europeans arrived,
sub-Saharan Africans were seasoned businessmen in the enterprise of human trafficking. It was only through a cooperative
effort between Europeans, Africans, and Arabs—that each side
saw as mutually advantageous—that permitted Europeans and
Americans to extend it to the West.

But why would the African indigene allow himself to engage
in this type of degrading transactional relationship in which
cheap costume jewelry and tawdry goods were used in exchange
for the lives of human beings? This book begins the examination of culpability and moral responsibility by looking at how
the African indigene made himself into a slave by adhering to
a primitive, philosophic belief in animism (an enslavement to a
cyclical, biological, and zoomorphic identification with nature
and the animal world) and the absence of a conception of an
appreciation for the intrinsic dignity and inviolate moral worth
of the individual human being as a human being. In other words,
the sub-Saharan bushman had no conception of the inviolability
and intrinsic value of human life and no political ideology or
moral system that could fight the onslaught of slavery.

The African indigene regarded himself as part of nature. The European, endowed with a Christian sensibility, saw himself as separate and apart from nature and viewed it not as a friend but as a phenomenon to be exploited—a thing that would adapt itself to meet his needs and desires. The African positioned as indistinguishable from nature, and the European viewed him as such. Concomitantly, as part of the expression of the Western personality, the European exploited *that* manifestation of nature and adapted it to meet his needs. The indigene, living outside the historical process, sentimentalized nature and adapted himself to it like all cyclical creatures who are, therefore, incapable of technological, spiritual, and cognitive evolution on a par with Western man.

Nevertheless, slavery was an egregious evil. Yet, in placing the African body into bondage and transporting it into the New World, European man simultaneously placed that body inside the historical process, and there began a torturous and painful induction into that process for those who came out of sub-Saharan Africa.

The journey would result in the violation of natural rights and of individuals' rights. Paradoxically, however, it would also result in the slow matriculation of the African indigene from being a natural creaturely personality to having a moral and highly individuated one that would value the inviolability of his own dignity and, through a yearning and struggle for freedom, come to conceive of the very idea of freedom itself.

If black Americans deserve reparations from whites, then every sub-Saharan African country that participated in and facilitated the trans-Atlantic slave trade owes reparations to black Americans, as do those countries from which the Arab traders emerged.

One sees how ludicrous this whole cycle is of attributing collective responsibility to nations and cultures for an enterprise that involved African collusion.

The fact is that reparations have been underway for blacks in the United States since its inception in 1776 and the creation of the Constitution. There, the moral framework for an abstract universal humanity was created. It was contradictory, ambivalent, and an on-and-off project until the Third Founding of America in the passage of 1964 Civil Rights Act (Lincoln's Gettysburg Address I submit, marked the Second Founding of the nation).

Since the passage of that act and subsequent post-1964 civil rights acts—the consequences of which lead to the first application of a moral eugenics program in the United States that sought to radically reshape the sensibilities of white people—reparations for blacks have been curated through various vectors of black socioeconomic, political, and educational institutions.

Despite the potential for a black renaissance—given the progressive society that we live in that is academically pro-black and one that inundates mega-corporations and small businesses with sensitivity training workshops, whose goal is to entreat whites to treat blacks with reverence and dignity—today, black culture is suffering from an existential despair and identity crisis. A cultural depression prevails. Since gaining freedom and living in what I will prove to be a post-oppressive age, many blacks whose identities were forged in the crucibles of virulent racism and deprived opportunities simply don't know what to do with themselves. Many see themselves as nothing more than economic supplicants. They are not inspired by the fact that, in the words of Robert Woodson, when they were in the grip of Jim Crow laws, had no political representation, and suffered gross income disparities to whites, they managed to maintain stable families, build hotels, create insurance companies, and owned and operated their own businesses. The elderly never had to fear any threat of harm from their grandchildren as many do today.

Today's race hustlers and nihilists do not point out, as Woodson does, that in the first fifty years after the Emancipation Proclamation, black Americans had accumulated personal wealth of $700 million. They owned more than 40,000 businesses and nearly a million farms. The literacy rate had climbed from 5 percent to 70 percent. Woodson in his book, *Lessons from the Least of These*, celebrates that black commercial enclaves in Durham, North Carolina, and the Greenwood Avenue section of Tulsa, Oklahoma, were all known as the Negro Wall Street.

Today, too many blacks are being resocialized under an anti-life philosophy that promulgates resignation, nihilism, Afro-pessimism, entitlement, separatism, victimology, misanthropy, and hatred of the United States as constitutive features of an authentic black identity.

For those who think reparations are their just moral desert and simply cannot get over the fact that they have been incrementally taking place for over 246 years now, I say: if the debt you feel has not been paid, then pray for the grace to forgive those you believe are indebted to you. You will come to know a peace you have never known, and you will embrace a feeling of freedom simply because you are free. Those whose lives had been marred by the ravages of Jim Crow segregationist laws live far richer spiritual lives by practicing radical forgiveness towards those who oppressed them than they would by seeking retributive justice. This is because an obsession with justice and entitlement shackles the soul in some sense to the compensations of the one who has harmed one. A spirit of aggrievement, paradoxically, places one in a dependent role on the other; in this instance, one is not free.

Radical forgiveness frees the soul from resentment and fosters an ethic of care towards those who have harmed one. Radical forgiveness not only forges new relationships, but it also heralds a model for a new type of humanity, a new planetary ethic, and humanism devoid of bitterness that will change the world.

To the black individual rising and striving to make something superlative of his or her own life, who refuses to be shackled by the racial script that would ossify the soul and calcify the heart, you are a historical process emerging in this world.

You know as I do that for this to happen, the race to which we were assigned must die so that the individual can rise.

The individual *must* rise!

ONE

Who Exactly Was to Blame? How the African Made Himself into a Slave

When European man and the African indigene first encountered each other, it must have been a shock to the sensibilities of both. Having established a particular relationship to the earth that differed greatly from that of the indigene, European man saw himself as more than custodian of it—he was its earthly owner who exercised divine dominion over it. He had done this by creating an abstract personality that had devised a method of exploiting and conquering nature to adapt it to suit his needs. He had divorced himself from his animality, transcended it, and placed nature in a subordinate position which he dominated and controlled with weapons, tools, and reason. Objects he encountered, including soil, trees, animals, minerals, and figures resembling human beings outside the historical process who presented themselves as part of nature, were treated as nature; they were simply appropriated, controlled, taken out of the state of nature, and commodified into socially useful artifacts for human consumption.

When European man encountered the African indigene, he did not discover one that was his military or technological equal. What he found was one that presented himself as irrevocably tied to his animal nature. The African indigene presented himself as a natural creature having not yet transformed himself out of biological time into historical time, from a conception of himself as a cyclical, biological creature into an epoch-making historical man. Indigenous man did not have these attributes; he was, literally, there for the taking, like the water buffalo, minerals and other resources that were part of his milieu. Had he transformed himself out of biological time into historical time, he would have devised the proper self-defense against conquest. European domination was made possible by the arrested epistemological development and faulty metaphysics of the indigene that allowed for his rapacious conquest. He was seen as existing in a fallowed state of nature.

Man becomes historical by creating new worlds that are symbolic and cultural in form with no formal spiritual animal equivalent. As an evolved being, he severs his spiritual ties with his animal past and engages in massive repression. Once man co-extends his animality into space and promotes and lives in biological time, his cognitive evolution, self-transcendence, and, therefore, self-maturation, are retarded. The celebration of his animal-self is fetishized. The animal within him needs no special encouragement. Rather, it is the birth of one who is self-divorced from nature and enters the historical process. A self that does not *make* this achievement will lose the battle to historical man.

Léopold Sédar Senghor, the black African philosopher, essayist, and the man who served as the first president of Senegal, writes of the African indigene as an animist at heart. He or she is one who feels linked to all beings—animate and inanimate. The animist for Senghor, who identifies with what he calls "Negro essentialism," takes care to adapt to nature so that all life, present, past, and future, is reverentially treated.

For Senghor, the African family includes the living, the dead, and the unborn. The dead and unborn are incorporated into family as totemic elements which can be living animals, carved wood, or even a plant. A clan may consider an animal or a tree as one of its members.

Human beings, in his view, are connected to other forms of life. Senghor believed emphatically that for two thousand years, with the exception of the Middle Ages, Western European man had mutilated man by opposing reason to imagination, discursive knowledge and reason to intuitive knowledge, and science to art. The African, he proclaims, has always known that to try to master nature is arrogant, foolish, and dangerous. Life is not to be domesticated.

Senghor believed that European whites and African Negroes possessed a difference that manifested itself in the cultural forms characteristic of each race. These characteristics are inherited; they result from the physiological makeup of the individual, which manifests itself in how each of the races develops their knowledge of reality. The African uses the body to produce emotional responses that allow the knower to participate in a kind of mystical union with the known. He, Senghor states, has no need to think, but to live the other by dancing it. To dance is to discover, re-create, identify oneself with all forms of life. It is, for the African indigene, the highest form of life.

European man perceives reality through perception mediated by mathematical logic, quantum mechanics, and a scientific approach. He typically visually discerns what is to be known and then attempts to analyze its basic constituents.

African man, on the other hand, goes beyond concepts, categories, appearances, and preconceptions produced by education in order to plunge into the primordial chaos, not yet shaped by discursive reason. The African's knowledge, Senghor thinks, is animated by invisible forces which govern the universe. They are harmoniously related to one another as visible manifestations of it.

This analysis by an African philosopher who claims expertise as both a scholar and a credentialed insider, as opposed to a dispassionate European anthropologist, is telling. I think that the problem with the African indigene was that he could not extend his imagination into a world that stretched far beyond his cortical range. Unable to construct powerful naval configurations that could dominate the high seas and go into extremely far-reaching territories, his physical, existential groping consisted of nearby raids and attacks close to the womb-like hearth where protective retreat into the zones of the primal tribe was always possible. He never learned to turn away from the ever cyclical and adaptive behavior of animal species and create colossal conquests of his own. Formal detachment and projection into an infinite future were absent from the range of his possibilities. Mimicry and imitation—whether of the ancestral world or animal world—are the ruling cognitive guides of the indigene.

Radical innovation would upset an unknowable order ruled by implacable and ineffable deities whose irreversible punishments would bring catastrophic designs on a people. The indigene's use of whatever semblance of reason he had was to divine the minds of the gods in order to placate and preempt them in their destructive and chaotic actions.

European man, by contrast, used his reason to justify and align his will with God's will. If he willed to conquer the majority of so-called uncivilized lands, then that was God's will all along. He has never truly feared God in the way the indigene feared his gods. European man was not a renter or a mere custodian and grateful equal opportunity dweller on and of the earth—it belonged to him, and he was God's representative on it. Period.

European man felt loneliness because of a detachment from his animality and his unsentimental domestication of nature. He placed himself above nature; he did not worship, extol, or venerate the creatures he willingly slaughtered, as do many New World indigenous peoples. He did not pray to their spirits for guidance, nor take on their likeness for deeper insight into an alternate reality. He, therefore, alienated himself from his primeval roots.

To attempt to recover the roots he had betrayed, he set out on a path of territorial conquests. These were symbolic homes for the hearths that he had abandoned, the roots he had severed, and the primal scene he had fled.

The conquests were not just a substitute for a discarded home within. They were signs of physical and spiritual potency and omnipotence writ large—the world was his home and belonged to him. Was this not the audacious belief of tiny England when it dared and did conquer and occupy one-third of the earth?

European man has always labored under the conception of himself as a post-human figure. Modern civilization was made by mandates decreed by God or by the rational construct of man's mind. European man, even when mired in tribal configurations, was always in flight from his roots to a large extent and, therefore, has always sought to forget from whence he came through explorative conquests. Unlike the indigene, explorative European man declared himself eternally independent and, in some degree, in contempt of primordial nature. For him, it is not only that nature cannot be sentimentalized—it must be commanded, subdued, and conquered. His governing philosophical credo was: "It was for me that this world was made."

To begin a historical process, one must often leave their origins behind and possess the hubris to act as their own *causa sui*, beginning a solo journey out of which they create a comprehensive mythology. They and their cultural milieu become the standpoint and the backdrop against which knowledge originates and against which the justification for moral action arises.

The African indigene was not written out of history by European man. His own cosmogonies canceled him out of the realm of high artifice that is a constitutive condition for being in the historical process. The subordination of nature and its radical adaption to man's needs is the juncture where history begins. The indigene's cosmogonies never emancipated him from the reality of flux and chaos to be catapulted into the epochal realm of mastery, domination, and conquest. It is not accidental that his dugout canoes and larger ships were never equipped to cross the high seas into Europe and conquer the British Isles. The cognitive feats of abstractions and mathematical computations required were absent, and understandably so, given what Senghor has described as the "African way of knowing and perceiving reality."

Perhaps they were missing because lacking in his thinking was a conception of a God who existed outside his creation that gave him cosmic significance and, more importantly, "cosmic specialness."

Every major conquering civilization has held and practiced a Manifest Destiny long before the term was coined in 1945 by

John L. O'Sullivan. It literally delineated the idea that the United States had a God-given right to take over territories all the way to the Pacific. As a noun, it was the belief or doctrine held in the middle of the nineteenth century that it was the destiny of the United States to hold its territory over North America and extend and enhance its political, social, and economic influence.

The term, however, may be retro-historically applied to European colonization and the African slave trade. We see the spirit and tenor of Manifest Destiny at work long before it was formulated as a formal, conceptual designator.

The African indigene had no Manifest Destiny. Not only was he technologically unequipped to carry out such a mission, but his cosmogony all but conceptually made it impossible for him to even hold such a possibility in his consciousness. If we query as to why African man did not colonize Europe or Asia as did the European nations, we will hear the facile answer that they were technologically not as advanced or that, given the challenging geographical oceanic and river structures and landlocked configurations of parts of the continent, they were unable to do so. Geography determines destiny, we are told.

Few would, I suspect, advance the naïve and idealistic notions that the Africans were a peace-loving set of heterogenous peoples given as they were willing and cooperative operatives in the Transatlantic slave trade, often selling their own people for cheap costume jewelry and trinkets passed off as precious metals by the Europeans. The question must be asked—why were they technologically inferior to the Europeans in the first place such that they were incapable of an expansionist, world universalist mission? The answer embeds another dilemma that implicates the indigene in the enslavement of his own people. He also lacked a conception of a moral personality—a universal "I"—and the concept of a juridical personality endowed with intrinsic dignity and universal, moral purpose.

THE CONSEQUENCES OF NOT HAVING A MANIFEST DESTINY

In returning to the question of the lack of a Manifest Destiny in the African indigenes, we see that they possessed no sense that the earth and nature were phenomena apart from their own natures from which they had to be freed. They were part of an amorphous, undifferentiated mass which failed to arouse a curiosity and wanderlust for anything beyond the proximity of their immediate sense perception.

All lasting civilizations are born of artifice. The African indigene resisted universal, civilizational imposition on others because, by living a cyclical and seasonal life imitative of the animal world, they compromised the capabilities needed to produce the skills required to leverage and vault the psyche over the horizon.

African metaphysics is one that deprived the indigenes from conjoining themselves with history. Enslaved to a non-transcendent, animal nature, it was, paradoxically, only by being enslaved that they crossed the threshold into the historical process. This tragic initiation awakened in the indigene the idea of moral and physical freedom.

In some sense, an expansionist doctrine can (but not necessarily) presuppose access to the reaches of God's will. Access to God's will bequeaths to one a transcendent ethos. In knowing the mind of God, one achieves epistemic arrogance, unknown to the African indigenes who function as supplicants to placate the desires and designs of a multiplicity of gods, inhabit their animal spirits and like foraging animals, always remain tethered to the earth. This is not the picture of the venturesome, cosmopolitan explorer roaming the high seas, facing the unknown, sometimes with fear and trepidation, but always moving with an indomitable and indefatigable will determined to forge a world of his own making.

One may object and point to the ancient Greek (Alexander the Great) and Roman Empires and ostensibly point to pagan gods under whose auspices geopolitical expansions were executed. Unlike the African indigenes who lived in fear of their gods, the ancients used their gods quite often as playthings, moving them as chess pieces to justify and rationalize their actions, rather than seeking to placate their unknowable desires.

The African indigenes held an isolationist, metaphysical cosmology. Non abstracted from nature, they were nonparticipants in a teleological progression towards high consciousness and elevated modes of being. To have achieved a level of high technological civilization required conceptual feats of abstractions that were not present. Societies that remained on the level of bows and arrows while others have transformed gun powder into high-level artillery and developed unprecedented navigational skills that qualified them to traverse one-third of the globe held different philosophies of life and a different relationship to the earth and the universe.

The indigene remains tethered to an animal nature. He is concrete bound and holds a perceptual level of acquiring knowledge. Higher-level concepts and the processes of abstraction is limited in him. However, in identifying with animal nature, the indigene's philosophical attitude was volitional. He wanted to remain a cyclical, purely biological creature.

Although the indigene had rites of passage that turned on heroic tropes within his local tribes and were validated via small-scale conquests of other tribal units within nearby compounds or at best, across nearby waters, these conquests and local discoveries never gave him cosmic grandeur or the universal, aspirational identity and consciousness attained by European man. His cosmogonies canceled him out of the historical process because they never equipped him to aspire to become a universal man—the measure of all things. Primordial cosmogony was always in flux and dependent on the weather, unruly demons, ineffable gods who ruled the cosmos, or tribal chiefs who had access to them and whose whims and moods determined the moods and nature of the gods themselves. Sorcerers and witch doctors were no rivals to scientists and naval and military innovators.

The African indigene was an animist, as Senghor proudly affirmed. However, unlike Western man, animistic man does not compartmentalize nor organize his world into tangible *things* that can be conquered. He hunkers into the earth and makes himself at one with it by mimicking the colors of the animals and environment around him; he inhabits the souls and spirits of the tress, plants, animals, and rocks and performs eternal rituals that vary according to a predictable cyclical pattern of events and occurrences that have become automatized in his subconscious.

We must remember that the African indigene (and numerous other indigenous animists across the world) attributes souls to abstract concepts, such as proper nouns, words, and inanimate objects, and cannot understand the differences between persons and things. It is, according to the founder of cultural anthropology, Sir Edward Burnett Taylor, an idea of pervading life and will in nature and a belief that natural objects other than human beings have souls. He suggested that it arose from early humans' dreams and visions and was based on erroneous and unscientific observations about the reality of nature. Taylor observed that the more scientifically advanced a society became, the fewer of its members believed in animism.

Psychologist and famed child developmental theorist Jean Piaget observed that children were all born with an innate animist worldview and anthropomorphized inanimate objects. He claimed that children would eventually outgrow this animistic belief and failure to do this resulted in a psychological and epistemological form of arrested human development. As we look at the Ojibwe people in Canada and others in Africa, we discover that personhood does not require human-likeness, but rather, a perception that humans are like other entities, including rocks and bears, plants, thunder, hillsides, and mountain tops. We then realize we are dealing, not just with a failure to achieve a scientific taxonomy that leads to at least a minimal achievement of concept formation and lower-level abstractions; we are witnessing the preconditions that make it impossible for animists to cultivate a robust and distinct human agency apart from their environment. This is not just a simple case of human beings being regarded as on equal footing with natural forces and plants and other animals; it entails the lower-level belief that even fungi exist as persons and that one should interact with them accordingly and with equal respect. In interacting and communicating with fungi, persons can, from the animist perspective, achieve knowledge that is otherwise unknowable.

Pervading the animistic world view is the idea that the group is more important than the individual; hence, collectivism is the unifying principle around which social life is organized. Every effect has a spiritual cause in which the dead and the living are linked, and ancestors play an active role in one's everyday life. It is like the world of the animal kingdom, a cyclical world governed by reproductive breeding. Traditionalism is paramount, and change, evolution and adaptation are secondary to the ways of one's ancestors. The continuance of said traditions supersede the radical changes required to modify and overcome the unexpected challenges of life and nature.

Undoubtedly, all cultures, civilizations, and societies need a philosophy around which their inhabitants can organize their lives. However, to advance to the level of a sustainable civilization, one needs a coherent, philosophic system out of which arises values, beliefs, and convictions that protect it against competing systems—and nature itself. Since this is not a work in comparative religion with a view to demonstrating which religious systems are more superior to others, I shall simply state a self-evident thesis: arrested development, which resulted from a strong adherence to and identification with animism, ill-prepared sub-Saharan bushmen for both colonialism and slavery. A predominantly oral and illiterate/preliterate segment of Africa could not have developed the epistemological tools that depend on a particular metaphysics of the world in which one has to truly perceive reality correctly to inoculate oneself against a mere subsistence level of living, poverty, geographic and cultural isolation, and ultimate conquest by a technologically and philosophically superior system.

Animism is entirely predicated on the primacy of consciousness over existence. This means that the individual holds his emotions, wishes, and desires as constructive of reality. Rather than viewing consciousness as perceiving an external world that exists independently of one's own the individual holds his as antecedent to existence and reverses the order by which it is known by a process of extrospection and awareness of the external world.

The animist treats the world as if it is a product of his consciousness and functions on the premise that if nothing existed, it would be a self-contained, irreducible axiom. It is not just that his world is illusory; it is that the animist has no way of hierarchizing the rudimentary and simple concepts he forms because there is no separation between his spiritual world and the material world. All exists in an amorphous and inchoate flux where the individual soul of a grasshopper is inextricably linked to that of the hills, his ancestors, and the birth of his newborn. He has no way of logically distinguishing unsubstantiated beliefs (that placating the rain-god-person with a sacrifice will bring rain) from the invariable laws of nature because the universe of absolute indeterminacy and flux has no counterposed system as we find in other religious systems to act as a corrective.

This manner of thinking had direct political implications. Unable to morally disambiguate himself from nature, the African indigene was conceptually unable to develop a moral vocabulary that could defend him from the rapacious pillage of European expansionism—an endeavor that the indigene was aiding and abetting. Responding to the stimuli of crass, short-term rewards analogous to an animal responding to a treat from a calculating master anticipating its cooperation, the African indigene lacked a sense of himself as a sovereign and autonomous moral agent made in the holy and sacred image of a transcendent God, one possessed of an inviolable and unassailable dignity. As such, he allowed himself to be exploited as a utensil and disposable tool.

To better understand this dilemma, we may draw attention to a moral and spiritual accomplishment forged in the registers of the first of the two Abrahamic religions and codified in Judeo-Christianity that gave European man another constitutive feature of his core identity. Having been made in God's highest *image* and endowed with His immutable attributes, European man had long emancipated himself from the status of being an object into one of a moral subject, existing independently of any description other subjects may have of him. God's interpretation of him had the imprimatur of moral indelibility and interpretive infallibility; he could be othered in the eyes of other subjects but not in the eyes of God. As such, the European subject could be made sense of and described without reference to his surroundings in an essentialist way. From an atomistic standpoint, his references were the attributes God suffused him with—his environment was simply the place in which he manifested them. The presence of "I will, therefore, it shall be" marks the characteristic of a moral personality that knows it is the bearer of moral rights bestowed on it by God even before a nation-state may have conferred such rights formally.

In this manner, European man had a moral framework, a horizon in which to spawn narratives that would allow him to make coherent, comprehensive sense and meaning and purpose of his life. The animistic pagan and animal-archetype of European man's primordial or phylogenetic makeup had long ago retreated; it was an anachronistic part of his psyche. He had long forgotten where he came from. He understood himself only by reference to what he had become—a self-surpassing, epoch-making, history-making, and transcendent figure. Possessed of personal identity, he established himself as a radical self-consciousness, self-perceiving, and highly individuated entity, who not only held nature in abeyance, but also in contempt as a necrotic amorphous mass that had to be conquered.

No memory bridge between *that* past and what he encountered when he met the African indigene was to be recalled. The animistic and animal-archetypal framework that he encountered rendered the indigene into an object outside the cosmic order and not affixed to any universal moral order.

There is no presence of the "I will" in the animistic personality. There might be primal brute force or predatory conquest that is episodic and spontaneous, but there is zero sense of an omniscient "I" acting under the auspices of God whose range of vision sees thousands of miles beyond the literal range of what is cortically possible. This European "I" is a cold abstraction that can be summoned at any moment to execute a plan of action, chart a course, and will a future to create history.

What exactly is the psychological state of men, who risk their lives on the high seas, armed with nothing but a vision to go beyond themselves, to surpass the imprimatur of the cultural identities that stamped them, the mores and norms of the tribe that formed them to ideate a new self and lose themselves in time and space on treacherous waters? Such men experience an essential part of the human condition that can be evoked and acted upon—the hunger to be more than one is, to forge an aspirational identity that allows one to surpass oneself. In other words, he wishes *to become*—to feel the lack and exigency in his soul and feed the wanderlust.

Exploration is a moral-creative act. Thus, the tragedy of the African indigene (and all New World indigenes) was that enslavement was forged initially in what started out as spiritual quests and a longing to fill a vacuum in the human soul.

What European man saw was not a recognizable moral creature who was translatable in his own cosmic mirror. What he saw was a *metaphor*. European man, through his Judeo-Christian identity, was an earthly deity, a transcendent phenomenon embodying a scientific, cosmological principle with an appetite for a fixed telos. He saw the African indigene as a flat-footed, earthbound, and concrete bound archetype. The birth and evolution of man is not man against restraint, not man in flight from something, but man soaring towards the transcendent—something outside of himself.

So, what is the metaphor that he saw when he looked at the African indigene? I submit that he saw an archetypal representation of something he had primordially inhabited in an earlier stage of his development but had transcended. He saw the metaphor of his shadow self; the science of biological, racial taxonomies had not yet been developed at the inception of the slave trade. So, we can be sure that European man had no Manichean, binary, normative terms affixed to racial identities. He conceived himself no more of being a white man any more than did Aristotle and Plato, who did not hold contemporary identities as white people. In fact, the term "white" did not appear in colonization law until the late 1600s.

European man did not initially enslave the indigene out of racist impulses. Rather, I submit that it was a primordial response to entrap and capture that which he had once been—primitive and in an arrested form of development. In his mind, the indigene had remained fossilized in time. He saw the self he had surpassed centuries ago, a self that he had to enslave, harness, and dominate lest he himself revert back to type.

The African indigene is his retrogressive ancestor, a phylogenetic trope, a regressive monstrosity he must harness and put to productive work to move him forward, lest he is pulled back into what he was and had outgrown, escaped, and evolved out of—tethered, enslaved, chthonian, and unabstracted from the earth. He masters that which had enslaved his humanity—the beast metaphor that stands before him.

In European man, we find an apex predator that came upon a broad swath of animistic, ancestral worshippers, many still granting fealty to mother cults. The sub-Saharans were, in the end, a people dominated by gynocentric paradigmatic models of living that rendered them a feminized and weak specimen to be voided and controlled by a master civilization.

The question of why European man did not annihilate the African indigene is left hanging. The shadow metaphor is strong. The very impulse to rapaciously conqueror and dominate is drawn from that primal and primordial reservoir embodied in the vitalistic African indigene, who is nothing but pure nature. Rather, he customizes that primal, raw vitality under a veneer of ideology and morality. He stamps it with the imprimatur of an unassailable axiom—civilization. In conquering the African indigene, European man, in his mind, was civilizing him by exercising certain attributes in his character that were regarded as moral virtues: vision, a venturesome spirit, achievement, glory, honor, transcendence, prosperity, productiveness, conquest, and undoubtedly, the capacity to vanquish.

Above all, European man would never be and has never been a victim of *cosmic injustice*. He saw himself as marked out with cosmic significance. Whatever private sense of alienation and existential angst might have marred the souls of men as individuals would be compensated for in feats of triumphant conquests that would translate into glory, prosperity, and wealth creation.

Slavery was forged in the tragic crucible of spiritual loneliness and European man's moral ambition to make something more of his life other than that of which he found himself the legatee and beneficiary. He stumbled upon human phenomena whose sense of life was different than his; often, a pastoral and bucolic existence of those who were fearful of leaving the hermetically sealed entombment of the continent—dread and fear, or an abject inability to experience existential loneliness in the universe, came at a cost. In never separating himself from nature,

17

the indigene felt at one with the universe and never suffered the chronic alienation of European man, whose very religion had made a clear distinction between himself and nature. For him, it was a thing to be commodified, exploited, and consumed for his earthly flourishing.

Judeo-Christianity had heralded a higher evolved consciousness in the psychic framework of the Western personality that elevated him from the earthbound and concrete state of a primitive savage to a transcendent being who now looked upwards at the sky—not just for inspiration and guidance but for an ever-expanding and limitless sense of how his capacious mind and consciousness could grow and approximate the mind of God. After all, God had made him in his own image. The idea of human perfectibility that philosophers like Jean-Jacques Rousseau and Immanuel Kant would expound upon were devoutly Christian ideas. In his encounter with the African (or any) indigene, Christianized European man was bound to find him as a non-recognizable and incomprehensible phenomenon.

In Christ all had been reborn, and a moral, egalitarian spirit pervaded the beings of all. The identity politics of Christianity translated into the biblical adage:

> "There is neither Jew nor Greek, there is neither
> slave nor free, there is no male and female, for
> ye are all one in Jesus Christ."

A metaphysics of redemption, hope, deliverance and, above all else, a radical, moral transformation predicated on a form of moral egalitarianism had become the new birthright of all persons. This metaphysics engendered confidence, mastery, and a belief in the right to conqueror the earth, as God had made man in his image. He was the fiduciary and custodian of the earth, which was there for him to flourish and prosper. If God had made man in his own image, and all were reborn through Christ, then the literal mind of God dwelled in each and every man on this earth.

THOU SHALL BE CANCELED THROUGH THE BODY AND BE REBORN IN THE SOUL

Christianity was a moral paradigm shift and remains the most audacious work in moral eugenics—the transformation of sinful and varied persons from a multiplicity of backgrounds into a single, homogenized Christ-soul. It was a historical and unprecedented paradigm shift in human history that has never been altered, undermined, or overturned.

However, that shift could not make those who had rendered themselves objects and had not yet transformed themselves from natural (animal creatures) into moral (transcendent God creatures with a moral personality and concomitant rights) intelligible. Indeed, the Christian missionary civilizational agenda was about the achievement of this attainable feat. European man saw a phenomenon standing before him—a natural creature informed by God to utilize nature as his material sustenance, comfort, and leisure, to domesticate it and to use it sustain and enhance his life, as he would a mule, oxen, water buffalo, or camel. Such a phenomenon, depleted of any concept of individual, moral autonomy and God-given rights with no technological prowess (save primitive utensils cut from nature), seemed no more distinguishable from a toad emitting poisonous froth from its back, a snake baring its fangs, or a tiger extending its claws.

As far as European man could make sense of it, *that* phenomenon was outside the pantheon of the human community and, *a fortiori*, the domain of the ethical. When critics of chattel slavery complain bitterly that the colonizers and slave traders did not see the African indigene as a full-fledged human being—they are absolutely correct. It is my hope that this dispassionate and philosophical-anthropological account will give an accurate description as to why that was the case.

The African indigene, with his idolatrous worship practice, and animistic and ancestral sensibilities, enacted this in a social system that included African/African enslavement that predated the arrival of the Europeans.

When frameworks that produce meanings and interpretations of the world are radically different, then the narratives that they produce are non-translatable. What one looks at, therefore, is not an enemy or adversary, but simply an unintelligible framework that exists outside the realm of sustained communication. One deals with such individuals in a piecemeal manner, both cognitively and transactionally. In human categorical terms, one looks at an *empty set*.

We face a question that must be asked honestly—did the Europeans, who engaged in the enterprise of chattel slavery, act from willful, evil impulses? For the 400 years that the enterprise lasted between Africa and the Western hemisphere, can we state with absolute rectitude that systemic evil drove the trafficking of human cargo? Or were there, aside from what has already been written, other mitigating circumstances that facilitated the trade?

We must remember that the beginning of African chattel slavery preceded all ideas of race as biological typology and the racism distinctly associated with them. These did not appear in

Western culture before the eighteenth century. This was partly because of the historical origins of modern biology.

In the nineteenth century, German philosopher Georg Wilhelm Friedrich Hegel noted in his magisterial work, *Lectures on the Philosophy of World History*, that slavery itself was a necessary stage in historical development made possible by the African indigenes themselves. He notes that, lacking any conception of justice or right, the African evinces a "complete contempt for man and a respect for life itself." He goes on to say that "slavery is the basic legal relationship in Africa," a place where the distinction between master and slave is completely endemic and accepted as natural. For Hegel, in a culture where human life has little or no value, the enslavement of Africans by Europeans is at least partially necessary on the premise that it can educate the African to have consciousness of his freedom. Hegel also admits that slavery is unjust; when slaves are brought into the domains of a rational state, their susceptibility to European culture makes them ideal candidates for manumission.

I take it that Hegel avers to the idea that—once in a rational state with all the infrastructures for moral and political matriculation—the slave eventually enters the historical process and begins an induction into resocialization and, therefore, retransformation, from barbarity into a civilized moral creature, aware of himself as a sovereign and autonomous man possessed of an inviolable, moral dignity. Since this transformative process could not be done in the state of nature through an appeal to reason and rational persuasion, the indigene had to be broken and denied freedom in order for a new consciousness to awaken inside of him—the idea of his own radical, moral freedom. It would require a long process; the socio-political stages would be circuitous and torturous, but the day would come when the manumission would yield a subject with an evolved consciousness that was suffused with concepts like justice, and political and moral rights and freedom.

The primary problem for the African indigene was metaphysical, then epistemological. He had never discovered the true nature of man or the requirements needed for his proper survival as a full-fledged, rational human being, largely because he had never discovered the true nature of an objective reality that existed independently of his consciousness.

If you have never discovered the true nature of human nature, you cannot discover man's intrinsic value as a human being, and therefore, you will not develop the philosophic system to protect him. A development of the proper philosophic system will mean that you build, over time, the right politico-economic and judicial systems under which the individual can also develop. It means that you are driven to develop a multiplicity of systems that protect the rights of the individual and whatever territory you occupy from foreign invasions.

European colonialism was made possible not because of the advanced military technology of the Europeans, but rather, because of a flaw in the continental structure of Africa, which was first metaphysical—a misinterpretation of the nature of reality. This produced an attendant epistemological or cognitive malfunction and the subsequent ethical and political egregious errors, all of which stemmed from a faulty perceptive apparatus. Such a state of affairs cannot give rise to advanced technological capabilities.

If human beings are not revered as individuals who bear a distinct identity in the cosmos apart from animals and inanimate objects, then there is no philosophical or psychological motivation by its inhabitants to defend the land or its people. As any sundry study of the slave trade reveals, the deals made between tribal chiefs and kings, Arabs, and Europeans in what is known as black Africa proves that humans were regarded by Africans as being reducible to fungible and interchangeable bartering objects. No moral group of individuals betrays its continental and regional peoples by first enslaving them for, among other reasons, being possessed with witchcraft. Animism, the primal and predominant religion of all of pre-slavery Africans, sees as much God in the human being as it does in the brass pans, the cotton, the guns, and trifling trinkets worth little in Europe. It holds this view while extolling equal value in a poisonous snake or the rotting carcass of a vulture to that of a human being.

To circle back to a Hegelian theme, the induction of the African indigene—and indeed, all pagan, primitive indigenes—into the Christian hemisphere was a purposive act on God's part to begin a process started in Christian identity politics. Moral eugenics is a process of achieving moral egalitarianism in which a self-evident truth—*all men are actually not created equal*—was made irrelevant. Some have an unequal share in intelligence, physical strength, and beauty. The reality—*all men are not born equal*—was reversed through an act of moral transubstantiation via the death and resurrection of Christ. Humans were regarded as equal in moral worth, value, and intrinsic dignity in the eyes of God. Such a truism would later be the moral insignia that marked the Declaration of Independence of the United States of America—that all men are created equal and endowed with rights by their Creator.

In another eschatological reading, it was part of God's purposive, long-term plan to bring all pagan indigenes into the pantheon of Christendom, which could be regarded as embodying the highest level of evolutionary consciousness.

In the end, how does one reconcile two antithetical viewpoints? One promulgates and enacts a worldview on the order of, "The world was created for me; the world belongs to me, and I to it; I came. I saw. I conquered." This was the ethos of European man. The other saw things differently: "The world was created by ineffable and malevolent phenomena who need constant appeasement. I am merely a renter of this earth who crawls upon it, more in fear than in masterly confidence. I was born; I cower in fear; I appease and follow a mandated script from birth to death."

The holders of one viewpoint possessed a Manifest Destiny that made them existential disruptors and creative forces wherever they ventured. One could say that the symbolic journey European man took in the thousands of miles he embarked on from home was indicative of the lonesome distance he felt between the place he started from and where he thought God must reside. The farther he traveled, the closer he might have imagined he would be in terms of proximity to God.

What he found was not unspeakable horror but simple remnants of a bygone era he had long transcended—domesticable, capturable, conquerable prey that, like the creatures that ploughed his agricultural fields back home, could be put to use with little resistance. They were not yet racialized creatures. Just commodifiable objects, extractable from the earth like minerals that could be modified and reshaped to his will.

If the indigene's will had been formidable, his forces of agency and civilization to be reckoned with his technological potency a spectacle to behold, then European man would have turned sheet white in terror and fled to the safety of his ships in sheer fright. Instead, he bestrode the continent like a colossus. Guided by the injunction that *that* land was part of the global commons allocated to all mankind by God and none was to be subjected to spoilage, all discovered resources were to be used and appropriated for the advancement of the species. With the indigenes presenting themselves as metaphysical inverts with no competing defense mechanisms, European man heeded his vocational calling and utilized the land and what he interpreted as its object-tools.

Africa valued slavery and is aid dependent today because it has never discovered the value of self-sufficiency or carried the notion of intrinsic dignity first articulated by the Stoics to its logical terminus. European-enforced slavery was possible not primarily because these small, militarily insignificant states were able to dominate an entire continent but because Africans allowed, endorsed, and were judiciously complicitous in the enterprise of slavery; they were not evil or intrinsically predisposed for enslavement. This was the case because they lacked a theory of inalienable, individual rights—a dignitarian repose akin to that which we find in Stoicism and, later, Judeo-Christianity.

Our thesis is that Europeans did not invent racism to justify the topical canard among the cognoscenti today. Instead, they exploited a continent rampant with tribalism and where factionalism and an absence of a general conception of individual rights, and a dignitarian approach to human life, were the coin of the realm. Racism, in the form of tribal demarcations among distinct groups sharing similar morphological characteristics, was already in place to European eyes. There were no invariable and categorical moral laws protecting the sanctity of individual lives from the evisceration of dignity or external attacks. Africa was not progressing toward a political analogue to the European renaissance or the imminent Enlightenment.

Instead, Africans presented themselves as fungible objects worthy of being sold to the highest bidder. It was the absence of philosophic protection that primarily left Africa uninoculated against the onslaught of enslavement and imperialism to which it was subjected.

Africa's biggest problem was never poverty, the absence of an advanced technology, or geographic and climatic unluckiness (Middle Eastern countries have built cities in barren "inhospitable" deserts). Rather, it suffered from an absence of philosophical coherence and consistency due largely to its absence of a civilizational schema and from its innumerable tribal makeup, which rendered it divisible and easily conquerable. With no sense of a strong state-centric consciousness, the continent was left open for nation-states with a unified purpose and goal—hemispheric conquest and territorial expansion—to exploit in a manner worthy of good hunters.

Who could have blamed the Europeans for conquering a continent of disparate and radically heterogeneous tribes of people with no conception of individual rights, the inviolability of the individual, no understanding of the intrinsic moral equality and worth of all persons, and no way of manufacturing patriotism and pride on a scale that would have prompted them to develop the artifices of rational protection against technologically and philosophically superior cultures with linear and well-defined objectives culminating in a rational telos?

Africa lay outside the historical process throughout history (and even to this day) because it lacked a proper humanistic philosophy. Indeed, it had varied religious traditions based on animism and philosophic folk conceptions. But because it lacked coherent written philosophical systems based on discursive reason, it was never able to develop a proper scientific method and, therefore, the discipline of science itself. It lags behind the West in the cultivation of rational inquiry and in world-historical processes and progress.

Africans have had folk philosophical conceptions consisting of bald assertions without argumentative justification. In a narrow sense, philosophy must have more than these. We may say that the non-discursive nature of folk thought is a drawback to progress and epistemological evolution. As Senghor states, the Western philosopher tries to argue for his thesis, clarifying his meaning, and answers objections known or anticipated, whereas the transmitter of folk conceptions says, "This is what our ancestors said." Therefore, folk conceptions do not develop over time. Given that the African philosopher writing today has no tradition of written sub-Saharan philosophy to draw upon, his plight is unlike that of the Indian philosopher, who may avert his mind to insights that might be contained in the long-standing Indian heritage of written meditations. He has classical Indian philosophy to investigate and profit by.

Twentieth century Ghanaian philosopher Kwasi Wiredu notes that a culture cannot be both scientific and non-literate because the scientific method can only flourish where there can be recordings of precise measurements, calculations, and observational data. If a culture is both non-scientific and non-literate, then in some important respect, it may be said to be backward. African philosophic folk conceptions are and have been historically based on a pervasive and systematic superstition and spiritism in which rationally unsupported beliefs in activities of all sorts have been advanced as human knowledge.

Today, the African philosopher has to conduct his inquiries in relation to the philosophic systems of other literate peoples who have well-developed systems of scientific and philosophic methods. The ancestors of today's African philosopher, Wiredu argues, left him no heritage of philosophical writings. In a deep sense, then, they left him no transmissible or conceptual moorings on which to leverage a sustainable identity, in the past, present and foreseeable future.

The African has no history; he has always remained outside the historical process, alongside the progression of other scientific and literate cultures. As such, he faced no unassailable bulwark against which to circumvent and neutralize the onslaught of the most magnificent of human civilizations or against any of what might be called its territorial integrity. If you don't inhabit written philosophic systems, then you cannot discover science and thus cannot protect yourself against the encroachments of superior types that are in the historical process and who, through their explorative ventures, aim to enhance their military, economic, and existential well-being. In the absence of a self-defensive African civilization, one can no more blame the Europeans for their conquering impulses any more than one can blame a magnificent lion from attacking and devouring the helpless and pathetic antelope on the plains of the African savanna.

Africa's major problem was not internal tribalism or domestic slavery, nor was it the expansionistic and colonizing endeavors of European civilization. Its problem was psycho-epistemological and, ultimately, philosophical. Its method of knowing was predicated on spiritism, animism, and on a preliterate sensibility that disallowed it from organizing percepts into concepts, which depends on the written word. The absence of a conceptual frame of reference and of a philosophic system that hold that schema in place is one that prevents the three essential registers of human survival from being discovered—time, savings, and production.

Historically, while many human civilizations joined the historical process, Africa remained not just outside of it, but congenitally incapable of ever joining it. When one's primary source of knowledge is intuitive rather than intellectual, one lags behind those who discovered the centrality and absolutism of reason and its connection to human survival, well-being, and eventual, sustained happiness—the highest moral purpose of any person's life. When one is looking to sorcery or the voices of human ancestors for moral and epistemological guidance and regards the quality of life residing in an insect as qualitatively equal to that of a human, one fails to philosophically and existentially matriculate from animality (or natural creaturehood) into moral human agency.

The central problem with the cognitive makeup of Africa (I am exempting Northern Africa, especially Egypt, from this category—Egypt is to be regarded as part of Arab civilization) past and present is that its inhabitants failed in the process of domesticating nature and, above all, abstracting themselves from it. Like the rest of the animal kingdom, the sub-Saharan African adapted himself to his background but never got beyond it. He also never got beyond the stage of adapting himself to the biological function of his body. To forge a civilization out of nature or command nature, it is not sufficient to simply obey it, which means nothing more than observing the invariable laws which govern it. Nature must be raped, exploited, and utilized selfishly for man's proper survival, which means a life of flourishing, the productive exercise of one's reason to the highest reaches of technological civilization, and the discovery of a political constitution that safeguards the rights, dignities, and requirements of human survival.

The mother cults in human societies reconciled man to nature and entrapped him in it; however, all great accomplishments in Western civilization have come from a struggle against human origins. The book of Genesis was a declaration of independence from ancient mother cults. And although mind can never be free of matter, it is only by imagining itself as such that human cultures can advance. We see that the Abrahamic religions were rigid and often cruel; however, they gave man hope as an individual in the sense that his transcendental God singled him out as special among all his creatures, and more importantly, gave him dominion over all living creatures on earth to utilize for his benefit. An unethical extrapolation of this creed came to apply to other men seen as inferior and lower in possessing a share in the divinity of God and the humanity of other human beings.

The genesis of Western man grew out of the crucible of the Abrahamic monotheistic religions and forged a distinction between the spiritual world and the natural or material world. In the process, man learned to domesticate God (He was on the side of human beings and their efforts towards survival) and nature, for which he was endowed with the cognitive capabilities to rapaciously exploit. This also wedded him to a mythology that saw his chief role as custodian over all the inferior or lesser types who inhabited nature. Trees were made to be felled dispassionately to make ships to conqueror lands; animals were not sentimentalized and seen as persons with their own unique spirit (a childlike tendency of all animists) but adversaries to be domesticated or slaughtered.

As Camille Paglia notes, civilizational achievement is a projection, a swerve into Apollonian transcendence. The desire to raise what started out as a primitive snout from the grub and nutritional minutiae of the forest floor gave way to a face lifted towards the sky and a projected heaven beyond it. That capacity for an upward glance gives one the evolutionary ability to speak and make utterances of meaningful communication to a God above. It is what allows one, for example, to divine they are a member of the chosen people of God, a status that allows them to forge the most lasting and enduring civilization and create a codification of laws through the written word that, to this day, is the backbone of ethical culture in the West.

Unlike other systems of religious thought or beliefs where people act contrary to their ethical prescriptive, animism is marked by a set of taboos and even totemic prohibitions. It lacks, however, centralized, coherent ethics, apart from some ineffable set of ecological, moral beliefs concerning how an individual ought to approach and eat animals and plants and interact with terrain. The lack of distinction between living and dead, immaterial and material worlds, and the interchangeability of personhood among animate and inanimate entities all leave individuals in the animistic world overdosed on spiritism, which, in the absence of a full-fledged moral system, renders them bereft of any categorical distinction between private and public, personal and institutional. The logical terminus of animism is ethical agnosticism with little hope among its adherents—in spite of other religious affiliations they might have—of achieving robust self-actualization, self-realization, self-transcendence, and individuated agency.

European colonial expansion out of which sub-Saharan European slavery began can be seen in several lights. One could say European man transformed each colonial outpost into an aspirational domain where any Englishman, for example, could realize himself and become who he thought he was meant to be in the world. These colonies were transformational units that, to the European cosmogony and moral imagination, were parts of a whole in a mechanistic, rational universe. Disenfranchised individuals were not so much regarded as social ballasts as they were inanimate parts of nature to be appropriated and transformed out of nature into commodifiable, material units.

It was on such terms that the New World was founded; the United States was the legatee of such a tradition. Paradoxically, in the seeds of its founding also lay the principles for the liberal emancipation of those who had been enslaved and left outside the historical process. It is to America's greatness that, beginning in 1776, she created a complex and often tendentious system that would eventually widen the pantheon of the human community to liberate and universalize those locked out of the domain of the ethical. It had built-in constitutive, regulative features of self-criticism, self-reflexivity, and self-correction. The road was messy, but the forward-looking intention of the principles was clear—all human beings were created equal. None today, in the United States, is locked outside of the historical process.

TWO

Fathers, into Thine Hands We Commend Thee: The Moral Meaning of 1776 and the Foundations of Black Freedom

The British had no issue with enslaving Africans and bringing them to the colonies that later became the United States of America. However, with the publication of the Declaration of Independence in 1776, something unprecedented happened in world history that would forever change the lives of those enslaved. A new American mind was born—a revolutionary mind forged in moral principles. It was the first time in human history that a country was created consciously through moral principles and via self-evident, axiomatic first principles. Over the next 248 years, these principles would socialize and resocialize the sensibilities of its citizens, forcing them to adopt certain habits of thought—a method of cognition about their fellow compatriots and their place in the world that would translate into specific actions. These would stir and torment the conscience of the men who inherited the institution of slavery, who knew slaves were, by natural right, deserving of their inalienable rights, endowed by their Creator, and that slavery violated the rights of human nature.

From the nation's founding until the Civil War that freed the slaves, American men—intellectuals, writers, politicians, religious leaders, and sundry men of simple, good conscience—would debate the heinous and despicable nature of slavery and how it ran afoul of the moral meaning of the country that had been founded. Economic and political expediency and their own prejudices did not catapult them into immediate emancipation of the slaves. The debates themselves did not produce the climate, the moral and political vocabularies, and judicial machinery that would eventually lead to the emancipation and freedom of those who had been enslaved and finally bring them into the historical process by admitting, as Thomas Jefferson did, that no human being is a natural slave or the natural ruler of another human being by means of racial identity.

One may say that prior to the birth of the American revolutionary mind, no other civilization that had exercised dominion over other humans came to hold such a belief.

In his 1773 pamphlet, "An Address to the Inhabitants of the British Settlements in America, on the Slavery of the Negroes in America," Benjamin Rush called slavery an unmitigated evil. In his magisterial and bestselling book, *America's Revolutionary Mind: A Moral History of the American Revolution and the Declaration That Defined It*, C. Bradley Thompson embarks on a brilliant and exhaustive account of just how the Declaration was instrumental in fostering a climate of rich and contested moral and political dialogue in the Union. He reveals the widespread abhorrence of many with regard to slavery, and the urgency to end it by such persons is made evident in his book. This held true even among those who were slaveholders, who fought a deep moral war within themselves over the sanctity of their moral identities and the values of freedom for all human beings that the Declaration stood for.

Benjamin Rush was not alone in believing that the newly formed nation inherited a birth defect in the form of slavery. Upon independence from Britain, he had hoped the slaves would be taught to read and write and instructed in business so that they could become self-supporting individuals. In Thomson's views, the abolition of slavery and emancipation were tied to the moral and social ideals promulgated by the Revolution.

Thompson points to yet another way the parallel currents in America regarding slavery produced a rich climate and new habits of thinking that would form the foundation for eventual black freedom and liberation from bondage. James Otis was one of the first American colonists to see the contradiction between slavery and the universal and unassailable truth in the axiomatic statements by Jefferson in the Declaration: "We hold these truths to be self-evident, that all men are created equal, that they are endowed by their Creator with certain unalienable Rights, that among these are Life, Liberty and the pursuit of Happiness."

In his widely read and acclaimed protest pamphlet, *Rights of the British Colonies*, Otis argued that every American colonist, white or black, is freeborn by the law of nature; he was emphatic that there was not any right by nature to enslave a person because he or she was black. Race, he declared, and the physiological features that go with it provide no grounds or logical inference in favor of slavery. He believed that the slave trade and the practice of slavery represented the most shocking violation of the law of nature. By that logic, he reasoned, blacks and whites born in the colonies that would be the United States were to be recognized a freeborn British subject—they were, therefore, entitled to the essential civil rights guaranteed to all men, as derived from the British constitution.

As Thompson eloquently argues, in the tenth essay in the *Federalist Papers*, James Madison made the case that an individual's unequal social status as determined by wealth, birth, and intelligence or moral virtue granted no basis for a lesser or greater claim to the equal protection of the laws. The Founders believed that government was created to ensure that the playing field was level and not artificially tilted to aid or hinder individual groups.

Thompson makes a strong case that every American revolutionary, including the ones who owned slaves, understood and accepted that slavery was an ugly, degrading, and brutal institution. None of the revolutionaries ever praised slavery as a positive good. Benjamin Franklin described it as an atrocious debasement of human nature. George Washington, who owned slaves, reported that there was not anyone living who wished more sincerely than he did to see a plan drawn up for the abolition of slavery. Madison declared that the superficial distinction of color made the most enlightened period a ground of the most oppressive dominion ever exercised by man over man. John Adams, who refused to own slaves as property, declared that he held the practice of slavery in abhorrence throughout his entire life.

The Quakers, who refused to own slaves on principle, published essays and pamphlets questioning the institution and its place in America. Some asked if the exercise of slavery could be reconciled with the profession of freedom that was founded on the law of God and nature and the common rights of mankind.

Thomas Jefferson owned slaves. He was, however, haunted his whole life by the pragmatic appeal to a principle of economic and political expediency on which slavery rested versus his own moral misgivings of the institution in which he partook. Despite holding contradictory views about the intellectual and cultural equality of blacks, Jefferson thought that such differences between blacks and whites existed within the white race and that slavery was a moral wrong because it violated the equality principle and the concomitant principle of individual rights. The relationship between master and slave was intrinsically immoral and corrupting. It was a form of despotism on the part of the master and a degrading submission of the slave. Slavery, he thought, debased everything that it met, including the slaveholders.

Thompson argues that almost all of America's revolutionary leaders, including those who owned slaves, hated slavery but were conflicted with the challenges associated with its immediate abolition. Chief among these was concern for the slaves' safety in a prejudicial society that was not yet ready to accept him as a free and equal citizen.

Abraham Lincoln, the greatest legatee and practitioner of the revolutionary mind, was determined to put the idea that the Union was not created to include blacks to rest and made a lengthy response to the assertion of Roger B. Taney, the Chief Justice of the Supreme Court, who believed strongly that the language of the Declaration did not intend to include Negroes. Lincoln was making slavery not just a moral issue, but *the* moral issue that would codify the moral meaning of the Unites States itself.

In my view, Lincoln wanted to close the contradictory and embarrassing chasm between the Declaration's claim to universality by its unassailable tie to the invariable laws of nature, and people who were clearly human beings but excluded from the domain of the ethical and human community because of physiological attributes. Lincoln declared:

> "I think the authors of that notable instrument intended to include *all* men, but they did not mean to declare all men equal *in all respects*. They did not mean to say all men were equal in color, size, intellect, moral development, or social capacity. They defined with tolerable distinctness in what they did consider all men created equal-equal in certain inalienable rights, among which are life, liberty, and the pursuit of happiness. This they said, and this they meant. They did not mean to assert the obvious untruth, that all were then actually enjoying that equality, or yet, that they were about to confer it immediately upon them. In fact, they had no power to confer such a boon. They meant simply to declare the *right*, so that the *enforcement* of it might follow as fast as circumstances should permit.

> "They meant to set up a standard maxim for a free society which should be familiar to all: constantly looked to, constantly labored for, and even, though never perfectly attained, constantly approximated, and thereby constantly spreading

and deepening its influence and augmenting the happiness and value of life to all people, of all colors, everywhere.

"I desire no concealment of my opinions in regard to the institution of slavery. I look upon it as a great evil, and deeply lament that we have derived it from the parental Government, and from our ancestors. I wish every slave in the United States was in the country of his ancestors. But here they are; the question is how they can best be dealt with? If a state of nature existed, and we were about to lay the foundations of society, no man would be more strongly opposed than I should be, to incorporate the institution of slavery among its elements."

Lincoln's speech is a *tour de force* in many respects. It established precisely what equality meant and did not mean. It put to rest the belief in metaphysical egalitarianism (prevalent today among the left)—that is, the idea that human beings are equal in capacities and capabilities. Lincoln knew that all men are, on one level, not created equal; this applied not just to blacks but also intraracially. We are not equal in intelligence, physical strength, moral sentiments, practices, virtues, beauty, perceptiveness, creativity, and a host of other endowments. We may blame nature for a sort of cosmic injustice in not endowing all creatures with equal, life-enhancing attributes or social factors that circumvent the actualization of those dormant capabilities that, if left open to cultivation in the right educational and socioeconomic environments, would flourish. Genius among the least of the expected could emerge.

America's tragic compromise made evident in Lincoln's speech was to assume that political expediency was a criterion for determining when such rights would be conferred on blacks and mistakenly believing that the state's role was to confer rights already granted by God and nature. The only proper function of the state would be to recognize such rights and protect them via unbiased judicial machinery that would make no distinctions about time, convenience, and the consent of those whom the society had predetermined on prejudicial grounds as being qualified to give their consent to be governed.

It would be unrealistic for Lincoln to demand that a group of uneducated, illiterate and culturally-lacking slaves could be regarded as his intellectual and social equals. By what standards? Of course, slaves, most of whom could not read or write, who did not have the leisure to develop their native intelligence, and further, for whom expression of such intelligence would be dealt with punitively, would be ranked as equal in relation to educated, aristocratic whites.

The metaphysical egalitarians of today advocate equality of outcome regardless of capabilities and an ability to control external factors that affect people's lives. Lincoln knew that personal values or attributes could not be distributed or reversed and that human beings who were superior in certain capabilities, either through natural endowment or social arrangements (no matter how unfair), could not be deprived of the result of their actions. Lincoln's speech is a bulwark against what is today known as "equity"—an abrogation of the Law of Causality by demanding equal results from unequal causes. In other words, one cannot properly require equal regards for unequal performance. The equality of all human beings makes sense only in the political realm.

But this level of inequality recognized by Lincoln was not a disqualifier from a deeper form of equality that superseded the natural inequalities among human beings. The genius and radical insight of the Founders lay in the fact that they were able to see that such unequal distributions were insubordinate to an undeniable moral axiom—that to survive as human beings, all had to be equally recognized as being endowed with inalienable rights to freedom, which is the precondition for carving out a life as a rational human being. Lincoln clearly realized that, comparatively speaking, whatever intellectual disparities might exist between blacks and whites, they were not ones that existed in nature, but rather, ones that were left as an open question; nature had mandated freedom, liberty, and the right to pursue one's own happiness. The framework of the new government was founded on the inherent moral laws originating from God and nature. Man had certain immutable, inviolable, and unassailable *hereditary rights.*

Lincoln's rebuttal to Justice Taney's belief that somehow blacks were outside the ambit of rights defends the metaphysical inequality argument—which by logical inference is intraracial and, therefore, should be equally applied to those whites who are inferior to other whites. However, Lincoln resists the social constructivist's argument by not saying blacks need freedom and liberty to develop their capabilities. The assumption is that even if freedom and liberty resulted in their continued inferiority, they are still entitled to their inalienable, hereditary rights. One cannot negotiate with the Creator and His laws and endowment of those rights on all his creatures, in whose eyes all are equally deserving of the self-evident truths postulated in the Declaration.

Lincoln was suggesting Taney was out of line. It was not his job to argue with God and his ethical mandates for man anywhere he was ensconced in a political demos governed by others. Self-determination does not rely on racial governance—it relies on abstract and universal principles applied equally to all. Laws of nature cannot be abrogated. Lincoln realized they had been delayed in the name of political expediency. What Taney was arguing for was not just blasphemous and metaphysically impossible. Debating with the invariability of laws of nature and hereditary rights to freedom and liberty as conditions of man's survival as a human being was, *a fortiori*, anathema to the moral meaning of the union itself.

To fight for the moral meaning of the republic, Lincoln would (with other reasons prevailing) secure the morality of the Union by eradicating slavery from its shores. The Civil War, regardless of the thousands of commentaries that have been written about it—its political significance, true meaning, and ultimate goals—was not primarily an altruistic act to free slaves in the name of their intrinsic moral dignity and inviolable moral worth. That it ended up achieving just that is not incidental.

The war, first and foremost, was an attempt to free America from being a moral contradiction in the universe. The United States was the first moral nation created by explicitly moral principles; therefore, that creation could not exist in violation of the moral axioms on which it was founded.

The *Gettysburg Address* was recited at the dedication of the Soldiers' National Cemetery in Gettysburg, Pennsylvania on the afternoon of November 19, 1863, four and a half months after the Union armies defeated those of the Confederacy at the Battle of Gettysburg. It is one of the best-known speeches in American history. Lincoln declared:

"Four score and seven years ago our fathers brought forth on this continent, a new nation, conceived in Liberty, and dedicated to the proposition that all men are created equal.

Now we are engaged in a great civil war, testing whether that nation, or any nation so conceived and so dedicated, can long endure. We are met on a great battlefield of that war. We have come to dedicate a portion of that field, as a final resting place for those who here gave their lives that that nation might live. It is altogether fitting and proper that we should do this.

But, in a larger sense, we cannot dedicate—we cannot consecrate—we cannot hallow—this ground. The brave men, living and dead, who struggled here, have consecrated it, far above our poor power to add or detract. The world will little note, nor long remember what we say here, but it can never forget what they did here. It is for us the living, rather, to be dedicated here to the unfinished work which they who fought here have thus far so nobly advanced. It is rather for us to be here dedicated to the great task remaining before us—that from these honored dead we take increased devotion to that cause for which they gave the last full measure of devotion—that we here highly resolve that these dead shall not have died in vain—that this nation, under God, shall have a new birth of freedom—and that

government of the people, by the people, for the
people, shall not perish from the earth."

In under 300 words, Lincoln managed to articulate the mag-
nitude of what no one could have imagined—a unified United
States of America that had ushered in a great Second Founding.
A fractured nation would have abrogated the axiomatic laws of
God and nature under whose auspices the republic had been
founded. Lincoln ratified what the Founders knew but could not
have affected into reality, as it would have cost them the republic
they were bent on forming—that contradictions in nature and in
God's laws do not exist. The Civil War was another installation
on an abstract formulation to formalize and make tangible the
reality of those floating abstractions that were not fully tethered
to reality. The founding principles would remain an abstraction,
so long as they were not applied to an enslaved people denied the
right to life, liberty, and the pursuit of happiness.

It would take another century and a Third Founding for the
republic to come full circle and for the principles themselves to
be totally grounded in the lives of all its citizens, but Lincoln's
speech is a religious one. Human enslavement was a desecration
of a significant portion of God's creatures. It constituted an egregious wrong that could reasonably be argued as a crime against
humanity. A confederacy of rebellious and seditious states living
contrary to the axiomatic laws of nature would have violated the
moral perfectionism at the heart of the creation of the United
States of America.

The Second Founding of America was forged in Lincoln's
Gettysburg Address to a nation conceived in liberty and the 13th
and 14th Amendments that abolished slavery and asserted equal
rights to all Americans was a universal, moral victory.

What Did the Founders Discover About Human Nature and Its Relationship to Politics?

Before we unpack that complicated moral victory, we must again start from the beginning. For if blacks are the beneficiaries of 1776 and the policies established from which they drew political and moral capital, then we must look universally and objectively at the revolution that was the United States Constitution. We must see the unprecedented feat the Founding Fathers accomplished to better understand exactly how enslaved blacks could one day be, not just legates of that tradition but full-fledged, existential heirs and successors of that tradition, which they can now pass on as a natural birthright to their children.

What I am going to say here is going to upset the moral sensibilities of many; however, it must be said. That the African indigene was subjected to the horrors of slavery was tragic. His forbearers bore as much responsibility as has been noted. Coequal blame and moral responsibility must be allocated between the two distinct groups. Once on American soil, however, his re-entrance into Africa did not seem tenable—notwithstanding efforts by both whites and blacks in the ensuing years to accomplish such a feat. Therefore, these questions must be examined closely—what political systems were set in place that did not have his full humanity in mind as a beneficiary or participant but were, nevertheless, configured in such a way that they paved the way for his future emancipation and full participation? Was the constitutional configuration of the newly formed republic one that would make it permanently illegal for the black individual to eventually become (albeit, through a protracted historical struggle) a full-fledged legal member of the body politic?

If the answer is in the negative, then we may say that there was—from the beginning of the formation of the republic—a preparatory stage for the black American slave to matriculate into a full, standing member in the domain of the ethical and in the pantheon of human community. As Thomas Jefferson noted about the slaves: "Whatever be their talents, it is no measure of their rights."

I want to return briefly to the early career of Thomas Jefferson. He had assumed a leadership role in pushing slavery onto the political agenda in the Virginia assembly and the federal Congress. In the 1760s and 1770s, he endorsed the end of the slave trade, and in his original draft of the Declaration of Independence, Jefferson included a passage that was deleted by the Continental Congress in which he blamed both the slave trade and slavery itself on George III. Unlike most of his fellow Virginians, Jefferson was prepared to acknowledge that slavery was an anomaly in the American republic and offered two practical proposals in early 1780. The first was a gradual emancipation scheme by which all slaves born after 1800 would be freed and their owners compensated. The second was prohibition of slavery in all the territories of the west as a condition for admission to the Union. His record on slavery placed him as among the most progressive voices in its elimination in Southern society.

The ensuing controversy and pushback to Jefferson's recommendations confronted a man who disliked confrontation. The relocation of black slaves to Africa or the Caribbean seemed logistically impossible. Unwilling to make the abolition of slavery a federal issue, Jefferson retreated to a moral compromise. Pushing for just treatment such as could ever be possible while men, women and children remained in bondage, he remained conflicted about the practicality of immediate abolition. He knew there was a contradiction between an aberrant institution and the philosophy of liberation he had helped author that was expressed in fifty-two words: "We hold these truths to be self-evident; that all men are created equal; that they are endowed by their Creator with certain inalienable rights; that among these are life, liberty and the pursuit of happiness; that to secure these rights, governments are instituted among men deriving their just powers from the consent of the governed."

Before moving on to the general principles of the founding of the United States in a manner that would eventually allow blacks to appeal to the liberal, emancipatory vocabularies and to equality found therein, we must grapple with another contradiction in the very founding of the nation itself; more particularly, the questionable reference to the three-fifths clause which referred to blacks as three-fifths of a person. There are numerous understandings of this account that range from it being an anti-slavery position that says nothing about the intrinsic worth of a black person to those who claim that it was a moral compromise to get the Union off the ground. There was, and could never be, anything pro-human about ostensibly pointing to a black person and identifying him or her as three-fifths of a person and claiming that they had intrinsic and inalienable and inviolable moral worth.

The origins of the clause were a debate between the northern and southern states over the issue of political representation. The South wanted to count blacks as whole persons—not for upholding their humanity but to increase political power. The North wanted them to count for nothing—not for rejecting their humanity but to preserve and strengthen an antislavery majority in Congress.

Those who argue that the Founders did not compromise on the Declaration principle that "all men are created equal" for expediency, and those who believe they did, reflect a grave misunderstanding.

Dinesh D'Souza has argued, for example, that the Founders were confronted with a competing principle that is present in the Declaration—that governments derive their legitimacy from the "consent of the governed." He argues that both principles must be argued and that, when they cannot be satisfied, compromise is not merely justified but morally required. D'Souza, without evidence, argues that the Constitution was pro-black and antislavery; he also believes that the three-fifths clause did not degrade humanity. "To outlaw slavery, without the majority of whites would be to destroy democracy, indeed the very basis for outlawing slavery."

One can only thank God that Lincoln disagreed. D'Souza's argument is not just of an apologist; it is bad moral reasoning. America, to begin with, is not a democracy. It is a constitutional republic in which the powers of government and citizens are strictly limited. Individual rights, inalienability, and inviolability cannot rest on the consent of the majority. No majority of any race, creed, or color can, for example, vote a person's property away. If all the white women in the union were subjected to gang rape as a crime for adultery and most white men voted to ratify it as legitimate, it would be a gross violation of their right to bodily integrity.

The problem here, of course, is that to have had citizenship and its rights imbued, one had to be legally classified as white, which meant one could legally violate the bodily integrity of non-whites. Because people already seen as white got to decide who was white, the unquestioned right of—in D'Souza's own words—white persons to determine the freedom of blacks went unquestioned. They were the ones legitimately governed; did they have a say in the consent? No—for obvious reasons. The circular reasoning leads to an illogical conclusion. Race, *simpliciter*, was the sole criterion of consent.

On the question of the three-fifths clause being compatible with upholding one's full humanity while one is still enslaved, I pose the question—has anyone ever seen a physical embodiment of a three-fifths person? How would such a person look? In all honesty, would it look like someone whose humanity and intrinsic worth would be recognizable? Would it resemble a person suited to inhabit a world any of us would recognize?

I believe that one must be honest and simply admit that, despite protestations to the contrary, there is absolutely no way an appeal to a three-fifths clause can endorse or appeal to a full-humanity commitment. It fails the reciprocity test *vis-à-vis* a comparison to the white individual, and it would fail the exchange test. This means that no white person would exchange his personhood status for a three-fifth share in humanity and be satisfied that his full humanity and personhood were still upheld.

We must see this as an emergent phase on the part of the developing republic to literally bring the African into the historical process on a painful and protracted level that, in and of itself, is demeaning to the black subject.

D'Souza claims that the Founders produced a constitution in which slavery was tolerated in deference to consent but not given approval in recognition of the slave's natural rights. Natural rights and enslavement cannot exist in the same moral system.

Frederick Douglass came to understand the wisdom contained in Lincoln's words against Justice Taney, and the gradualist approach to freedom contained in the Constitution itself, when he declared that slavery was "scaffolding to the magnificent structure, to be removed as soon as the building was completed… Abolish slavery tomorrow and not one word of the Constitution needs to be altered."

What I believe we must do is leave aside the question of slavery and black disenfranchisement and look at the larger elements that give rise to the founding of America itself—constitutive principles that would undergird the emancipatory movements of oppressed groups, including blacks, women, and the LGBTQ community.

The founding principles themselves are *the* moral and political emancipatory vocabularies that Martin Luther King Jr. appealed to and from which the Civil Rights movement derived much of its moral traction and political currency. The Founders, despite their compromise about slavery, got what I call the *fundamentals* correct; they would eventually bring all black persons within the historical process. This discovery of the fundamentals would see the liberation of black agency and allow blacks to flourish and compete with whites, even in a world that continued to remain hostile to their creative endeavors. The ability to overcome such obstacles was because of the very way America itself was constructed.

In the ensuing pages, I will demonstrate how in, the creation of America and its seeming obliviousness to black sovereignty, the republic created the political architecture in an abstract and universal manner that blacks would inherit for their eventual, total freedom. In those universal and abstract configurations they would be socialized into the civilizational mores of American societies and become *Americans* in the various processes and iterations that constitute Americanism and Western civilization. They would find the substratum of their freedom in the moral revolution that created the United States, even though the revolution might not have been explicitly declared in their name. In fact, what made the nature of that revolution so extraordinarily unprecedented was that it could be later expropriated on moral terms by disenfranchised persons from various groups. These individuals would find its universal language of inalienability and hereditary rights for all as equally belonging to them as individuals. They just happened to be unfairly singled out and targeted for immoral discrimination as members of an unprotected class.

On the plantations, with their agency heavily compromised and legally restrained, blacks could not fully enter the historical process. They could not yet matriculate out of a process of primitive and restricted intellectual development into fully civilized agents. That would start with their emancipation. It is irrelevant as to whether the emergent republic had them in mind as future, full-fledged members.

I have made the case that two concurrent, parallel societies on the issue of freedom for blacks and their inclusion in the republic existed. One championed inclusion and freedom, while the other focused on exclusion and continued disenfranchisement. The ambiguity around black equality was not anomalous. In the end, the moral and political vocabularies and the sociopolitical machinery that formed the republic was one that was generative. It propelled itself into an indefinite future in which blacks would be the legatees and beneficiaries.

Let us now turn to the abstract revolutionary nature of the republic and the moral systems of thought that drove its formation.

A Revolution in the Human Soul

When the Founding Fathers turned on the light of reason over 244 years ago and wrote the Constitution and Declaration of Independence, they achieved a remarkable feat. It was not just, as hundreds have remarked, the creation of an unprecedented political achievement that was the constitutional republic of the United States of America. This republic, replete with its Bill of Rights and subsequent constitutional amendments, was a major civilizational advancement over any other political phenomena that had ever existed. But the major achievement of the Founding Fathers was not political; that was a derivative achievement. They, the first and last of America's great intellectuals, had done what no other philosopher had done in the history of mankind.

They achieved a revolution in epistemology by discovering the proper application of human nature to its appropriate political configuration. For the first time, the requirements of man's survival *qua man*, that is, man's nature as a rational and conceptual being, were grafted onto a social and political environment that supported its rational upkeep. The political milieu that they created was a direct corollary of that nature. In other words, they were the first to understand that the teleological endpoint of all human striving—freedom and happiness—required a specific political milieu in which human preservation and the achievement of rational happiness were possible. They were the first to integrate man's nature with the perfect political environment.

America was and remains a metaphysical concomitant of human nature, *simpliciter*; it is a metaphysical expression in the form of a political republic derived from an unprecedented epistemological feat—the perfect integration of a discovery of man's nature and the *artificial creation* of a political system that corresponds to that nature. Until the founding of the United States of America, the history of humankind had been replete (and continues to be) with tragic experimentations in what I shall term *political epistemologies*, or the attempts to find the right political system consonant with man's nature as a conceptual and rational being. The results fell short of the type of life suitable for a rational being, a life that transcends mere preservation and survival to include the possibility of one that embraces flourishing and thriving. Nomadic wanderers, primal tribalists that made no distinction between animal and human life, despotic theocracies, secular dictatorships, rulership by divine order, majority-ruling democracies, and rule by medieval warlords had all failed to realize that negative liberty and absolute freedom to create a conception of the good for oneself were the fundamental requirements of human nature, morally and existentially.

In the bad cases of human history, politics had always preceded and superseded morality—by default or in deliberate ignorance of the proper requirements of human nature, human beings had devised political systems that did not correspond to the objective and rational requirements of conceptual and rational beings, who had to live by reason and the judgments of their minds.

The men who devised such systems, from the most primitively tribal ones dominated by hordes to the most exalted of their time such as those formulated under the Roman Republic and Empire, had never sought to question the moral foundations, precepts, and principles that legitimized such systems and made them valid. They never sought to discover that what made a political system valid was the degree to which it corresponded to the requirements of the individual as an individual. A system that secured the rights that protected the conditions indispensable for human self-preservation, flourishing, and the achievement of the end of all human striving had never been properly founded. A political system defended and devised via moral means that secured the achievement of a rational form of happiness that was not based on arbitrary whims, emotions, or desires that could short-circuit the well-being of the individual in the long-term had never existed before the conscious founding of America. America itself was conducive to a form of political happiness that secured the individual's long-term security, well-being, and flourishing. This enterprise belonged first not to politics but to the science of ethics—a science that could discover, with a high degree of accuracy, the virtues and method of cognition suitable to the life of a human being. The translation of this discovery into an organic and material social application is what we may describe as a political system. Without the proper morality, political systems are doomed to fail. But without the proper epistemology, or proper ethical and moral system, values and virtues remain obscured from the realm of human cognition.

When Thomas Jefferson declared: "We hold these truths to be self-evident, that all men are created equal, that they are endowed by their Creator with certain unalienable Rights, that among these are Life, Liberty and the pursuit of Happiness," he achieved a revolution in epistemology. His perception of self-evident moral axioms did not stop at the above proclamations. He extended his list to include the purpose for which "Governments are instituted among Men," the insight that governments derived their "just powers from the consent of the governed," and "the Right of the People to alter or abolish" an unjust government.

Yes, Jefferson did view all these truths as epistemologically self-evident. He did not intend them to be accepted with argument or further demonstration. This was a mighty feat of epistemological abstraction. To have derived from the Right of Nature which posits man's self-preservation as both a biological descriptor and a normative duty to protect such a life, Jefferson and the Founders perceived the corresponding social and political existential corollaries. We should not, as some have suggested, regard self-evident truths in a practical sense. To perceive something as self-evident is an epistemological function; it means to grasp an irreducible primary as a single unit and, with lightning and brilliant speed, to see the corresponding social requirements for life, liberty, and the pursuit of happiness (equal counterparts) almost automatically. All the self-evident truths were moral axioms deduced from human moral nature.

It is the correct grasp of human nature that led to the infallible, sociopolitical, existential corollaries in one's cognitive, epistemological feat. Any practical application of the self-evident truth is logically posterior to such truths. An application of a precept of reason presupposes the first discovery of the principle via an epistemological route.

Thus, we see that the birth of the United States was one formed in the matrices of a practical philosophic system. It was the first nation forged by consciously held philosophical principles in whose application no breach between theory and practice was entertained. It would be too conceptually broad to state that the United States was created as the first philosophical state. That declaration would not be untrue. It would not, however, capture something fundamental about the new republic. It was the first consciously created ideological state.

Other civilizations, such as the Greek and Roman, were guided by explicit *de facto* principles, as have been the cases with communist, socialist, and fascist governments. America and its civilization were literally formed by the conscious discovery and application of an explicit political philosophy. America's political philosophy—its ideology—is a constitutive feature of the civilizational identity of the republic. Without them, America would exist as a geographic entity demarcated by state lines. It would cease to be America, *simpliciter*. Its *de jure* founding principles form the core of its political and public culture. It is the foundation which undergirds citizenship and civic identity. But the realm of philosophic abstraction and of social and political reality are expressly integrated by the revolutionary nature of government devised by the Founders. Without the latter, there would have been no way to have tied philosophical principles into concrete reality or into actions guided explicitly and consciously by ideas.

Thus, Americans became the first people in history to—consciously or unconsciously—live by holding an explicit philosophy of life. A robust political philosophy that constitutes a nation's political ideology plays a subtle role of cultivating what we will call civic virtues that cultivate habits of thinking and, thusly, a particular kind of behavior in the public sphere. Such virtues, if only thinly informed by the political principles, still pay explicit attention to the sociopolitical characters of its citizens, what we may call the *public face of Americans*. That public face was legitimized to the extent that it was grounded in rational principles.

This is not to say all Americans were rational or moral, but those who chose not to live by the dictates of reason—that is, outside the realm of an objective reality—were (and still are) regarded by the very design of the American system as cognitive and social ballasts. They would be free to avoid reality but not free to evade the consequences of avoiding reality.

We may say that the Founding Fathers were fundamentally driven by a moral vocation, not a political one. That they produced a scientifically valid political document was a metaphysical concomitant of their antecedently held moral principles. Their moral sensibilities translated into the concrete realm of action resulted in a political system that, in and of itself, is a moral system. The Founding Fathers could not have established the proper political system suitable to human preservation and long-term survival without discovering and understanding its moral foundations that granted it its legitimacy. And since ethics is a derivative of metaphysics and epistemology, they would have arrived at the correct metaphysical and epistemological procedures before being able to conclusively and immutably understand the political requirements and attendant system for the indefinite upkeep of man's moral nature. Hence, they were comprehensive revolutionaries in the major branches of philosophy—ethics, politics, metaphysics, and epistemology.

What type of ethos and mindset equipped them to arrive at the correct moral, political, epistemological, and metaphysical systems that would result in a Constitution that so aptly matched the nature of man?

A New Sense of Life Shapes an American Way of Thinking

The answer lies in what we may term their *sense of life*. Philosopher Ayn Rand, who defined the term philosophically, described it as a preconceptual equivalent of metaphysics. It is an emotional and subconsciously integrated appraisal of man and of existence. It establishes the nature of a person's emotional responses and the essence of his or her character.

Before individuals are old enough to grasp a concept like metaphysics, they make choices from value-judgments. They have emotional experiences and acquire a certain implicit view of life. An individual's choices imply some estimate of herself and the world around her including her ability to deal with the world she encounters. To the extent that an individual is mentally active, which means she possesses the desire to know and understand, her mind works as a programmer of her emotional life. As a result, according to Rand, her sense of life develops into a positive counterpart of a rational philosophy.

The main concept in the formation of a sense of life is the idea "important." Since the term belongs to the realm of values, one can surmise that that which is important establishes the base of ethics. There can be no such thing as unimportant values or values that are bad since, by definition, they are life enhancing phenomena. One can no more hold a bad value as one can properly hold something that is falsely important. People may be mistaken in their beliefs about what constitutes a valid value in their lives, as someone who claims that injecting heroin is valuable to him and the opiate a value in his life. Here, we would claim that the person has a definitional problem—he has misapplied usage of the term to describe a thing in life that he believes is important. A drug addict may claim heroin as a value in his life; however, for "important" to have a proper application to the life of a rational person, it would have to constitute a real good.

The integrated sum of a person's concept of what he *thinks* (rightly or wrongly) as important and valuable is his *sense of life*. For Rand, it represents a person's early value-integrations, which remain in a fluid, plastic, easily amendable state, while she discovers knowledge to arrive at a consciously directed process of cognitive integration. This means she arrives at and lives by a *conscious philosophy of life*.

We may say that living by a conscious philosophy of life is the most mature expression of a sense of life. It is the explicit validation of one's values translated into a comprehensive and well-integrated form of philosophical stylized living. It involves translating into fully conceptual terms the emotional approximations and appraisals by which a person has lived. It means going from living and experiencing the world from a wordless, feeling-bound form of existence into being led by a rational and conceptually valid road map that will direct the course of one's life.

What, then, was the sense of life of the Founding Fathers that may be established against the preceding definition? What emotional projection did they enact upon the universe, and how did the ethos they each commonly held translate into a rational philosophy of life?

I believe that the Founders held a passionate love for man and this earth. The most blatant expression of their love of man was to be found in the recognition and defense of him as a rational and autonomous, sovereign individual and all that was entailed in the recognition and affirmation of this truth—that he was deserving of life, liberty, and the pursuit of his own individual conception of happiness. Their love of man took the form of a deep respect for him, such that he should choose his own conception of the good life for himself with the explicit understanding that it was impermissible for the state to regulate, coerce, or encourage one conception of the good life over another; each man, based on a rational observation and analysis of his station in life and his values, was to be left alone to determine what was good for him and his life. It was no more the business of the state to tell a man whom to marry or whether to marry, whom to worship or whether to worship at all, than it was his neighbors' business to do so.

The discretionary power to choose from a broad array of values was his and his alone. The Founders started with a civic love for humanity and man that they translated via a political system that secured the individual rights of each person. The rights, which secured moral axioms of life, liberty, and the pursuit of happiness, were as unassailable as the moral axioms themselves.

Their exalted sense of life finds its proof not only in the respect for man's sovereignty and his rightful place on earth as an autonomous agent who had a moral property in his body, labor, and mind but also in their belief that metaphysically speaking, this was to be man's heaven on earth. Their proclamation of man's inalienable right to the pursuit of happiness was a reversal of traditional Christian rejection of this earth and this world and the idea of suffering as man's proper existential fate. Happiness was man's natural end, and this earth—not heaven or some ineffable notion of an afterlife—was the place where he could successfully achieve it.

The theological implications of this philosophic system were vast. Despite the theistic commitments of many of the Founders in creating a secular nation in which the state could establish no formal religion, they were the first political eugenicists in recorded political history. The American man or woman was to be the prototype for a new type of human being—one who needed no redemption, no religious atonement and/or salvation. Reversing the mythology of Edenic man, America was its own Edenic paradise where the new and first people could achieve happiness and fulfill their purpose and meaning right here on earth. The Founders of a consciously created secular nation where the primacy of the individual supersedes that of faith, church, and even God are not those who—protestations to the contrary—believed in the concept of man as born with the stain of original sin. Their actions in the creation of America spoke louder than any of those among them who were Deists.

Unlike their historical predecessors who had terrorized man, sought to rule and coerce him, and subordinate him to the wishes and whims and fiats of society, the Founding Fathers saw men as their metaphysical equals, with each possessing no greater share of humanity than any other and with an equal apportionment of moral value. Indeed, it was this recognition that would be the moral foundation for the emancipation of slaves and abolition of chattel slavery, which they did not create but inherited from the old world.

The Founders, many of them aristocrats, were able to abstract from their own material status and project a benevolent ethos towards all human beings in general, largely because they saw that the concept of the indivisibility of man could only be guaranteed through his enouncement in a constitutional republic. The republic they devised was not based on lineage or blood, nor would citizenship be tied to bloodline or nativism indefinitely; in fact, it was quite the opposite. Their love of man and of humanity was forged in a visceral dislike of tribalism—the very mindset which had characterized the old world and under whose tutelage they had been socialized culturally. It is obvious from the spirit and law of the Constitution they created that they saw America as an open country, one that would be populated by strangers and foreigners from a broad phalanx of peoples. Such individuals would retain their cultural specificities if they so desired, but they would be united under a common core rubric of republican values that would give them all a common, unassailable public identity.

Unlike their historical predecessors and moral counterparts, the Founders' sense of life was one that attempted to solve the problem of man once and for all and, concomitantly, the nature of existence. With rare exceptions in human history, man had always been conceived of as a problem to be solved, overcome, or via a curious mélange of religion and social collectivism, something in search of justification for his existence, redemption, atonement, and salvation. Those who did not believe this, such as Aristotle, condemned man to such a fate by failing to create a political apparatus that would have reversed or annulled such a view of man by virtue of the system of politics under which he lived.

The Founders projected a sense that reality was to be perceived and mastered correctly through observation and comprehended via logic and reason. Theirs was an ethos of confidence that translated itself into action that yielded results coterminous with human achievement, success, and joy on earth.

The Constitution that they created was both a ratification of human nature and an implacable inoculation against the nefarious forces of man to assault the physical integrity and the mind of man. When Jefferson stated: "I have sworn upon the altar of God, eternal hostility against every form of tyranny over the mind of man," he was uttering an ode and a love letter to the inviolable and indubitable characteristic that marks man as man—his rational, sovereign mind. Respecting the moral precepts of natural law translated into moral civil laws that subordinated the masses came as close to loving humanity as the Founders could in literal terms.

The sense of life of the Founding Fathers and their attendant love of man spawned from it, along with the universal, cosmopolitan, non-tribal, affiliative means of belonging in the republic, drove them to create a moral and political scientific document that formally ratified man's nature qua man—that is, man as a rational and conceptual being. Human beings had always looked for the true nature of man—that substratum that underlay the journalistic minutiae of his ordinary life and marked the incidental characteristics of his human personality. Aristotle may have discovered the true nature of man qua man, via his positing of rationality as the true essence of man and his Law of Identity, as an epistemological method of validating the discovery of that nature. However, even he failed in his attempts to create a corresponding political system and social milieu to accommodate *that* specific type of human nature. His political system was little more than a validation of the provincial Greek city-state that found its legitimation via majority-ruled democracy that kept many, if not most, human beings outside the domain of the ethical.

Civilizations within the historical process and outside of it had struggled to find a political system suitable for the requirements and rules of man's consciousness and nature. Rather than create a political system that ratified human nature and suffusing it with social inoculations against its integrity, the history of human political systems was complicated, from European despotism and absolute monarchical rule that subjugated man's inviolable mind to the whims and caprices of kings and queens to the Asiatic dynasties with their feudal systems and ineradicable systems of social hierarchies that trapped persons into birth-to-cradle social roles and stagnant identities, the tribal and nomadic hordes of Africa, and what is today the Middle East and indigenous populations. None advanced beyond the level of brute and feral animality or the psycho-epistemology of the concrete-bound range of the moment forms of existence. Those outside the historical process had neither discovered the proper nature of man nor a political counterpart to accommodate it. Even societies boasting of advanced civilizations, such as Egypt, still lay outside the historical process. Their systems of governance lay deep at odds with the essential freedom required for human well-being.

It is not surprising that Greece, the cradle of philosophy and, therefore, the proper methods of human cognition, gave rise to the beginnings of what would serve as the root of America's modern constitutional republicanism—democracy. This system would later be advanced and codified under the Roman Republic and Empire and spread via conquest and annexation to previously uncivilized countries, regions, and peoples outside the historical process. It is not surprising that—having discovered, formalized, and codified the proper epistemology and method of cognition as well as the proper nature of man—Aristotle, the metaphysical and philosophical father of America, would go on to tutor Alexander the Great, the first political cosmopolitan with a grand and unprecedented vision not to conqueror and destroy for the sake of plunder, but to unify the barbaric world outside the realm of history and bring it into the fold of reason, integration, and whatever semblance of progress the he and the Greeks might have possessed.

If we return to the sense of life of the Founding Fathers, there is much more to be said about their unusual political achievement. On one level, they had solved the problem that had haunted humanity since its recorded history. Man's fundamental problem in the world was not metaphysical or even existential. Somehow he had found a way to address these questions regarding the purpose of his existence and the meaning of his life through primitive religious systems that were beyond the pale of truth or falsity and testified more avidly to psychic expediency—that is, to the sense of whether it placated his insecurities and fears and satiated his need for some sense of mastery and control over his environment and destiny. Man had presented himself as a problem to be solved, one who possessed a being that had to be overcome, transcended, or tamed.

But his fundamental problem, before he had even fully grasped the essential and fundamental characteristics of his own nature, was political. He always needed a system that would safeguard his nature as a human being. Historically, man had created cages or erected walls and towers to cage himself and his fellow creatures in. The sense of life that spawned such systems was malevolent. It was based on the premise that man was a nasty, brutish thug whose nature and unruly sensibilities had to be harnessed. Even Aristotle could not have conceived of the Greek polis as a home to any outsider; only the civilized members of the polis, born and bred according to its mores, could claim right of membership.

The Founding Fathers were the first to create a vast open space in the name of unbridled freedom and set man free to roam upon it, to exit if he wished, and to return if he so pleased. They did not see man as fundamentally depraved or tainted by some ineffable original sin that corroded and corrupted his fundamental nature. They were the first to break a graven and erroneous view that all societies and civilizations had held—that man was a reducible product of his environment, determined not by his free will, rational desires, goals, and aspirations. The Founding Fathers, unlike those who especially had lived outside the historical process, did not hold to the view that what was good for their anthropoid ancestors was good for them. This was what the ancient Egyptians believed for more than a thousand years in one of the most cult-like, quasi-civilizations that had ever existed. It was, in the end, a cult predicated on the worship of death.

The Founding Fathers held that man deserved to be free because of the phenomenal spectacle that he was and because—at the heart of the moral foundation of their political Constitution—was the benevolent but morally proper conviction that *man qua man*, if he were to survive anywhere on earth, had to exist as an end in himself.

Man was not, metaphysically, an imminent threat to himself. He was someone who deserved to have the sanctity of his life protected by non-punitive rules—negative liberties that consisted not in what he had to do but what he ought to refrain from doing regarding the well-being of his fellow compatriots. These prohibitions only constrained actions that violated the inalienable, individual rights of others. As such, their laws were not designed to curtail creative agency and imaginative capabilities—in fact, quite the opposite. It set the individual free on a course of limitless activities that would lead to unprecedented achievements from which all would benefit. In writing this scientific document with an apparatus that corresponded to human nature, the Founding Fathers committed a moral act.

Such a magnificent sense of life could not just have produced a culture; it spawned a new civilization—the American civilization, which achieved an unassailable, ethical mandate in individual rights.

Immanuel Kant had claimed that the laws of logic, like all human knowledge, have no basis. In deriving his epistemological approach primarily from Plato, who regarded concretes perceived by the senses in the material world as shadows, he believed human concretes (i.e., individuals) also had to be regarded as shadows. Because the Platonic theory of knowledge—notwithstanding

Aristotle's monumental breakthrough—had dominated human cognition for several millennia, it colored the ability of all to see man in his totality or, more precisely, as a thing in himself, apart from referencing him by way of some noumenon realm. If man's nature lay obscured from human observation and perception, he would never get his just deserts politically or morally because the fundamentals of his nature would be occluded by a method of cognition that deliberately cast off his perceptual apparatus as incompetent and incomplete.

The Founding Fathers were the first to truly get man right—notwithstanding John Locke's magnificent recognition of who man was by nature and the requirement of property as an extension of his rational capacity to produce on behalf of his survival.

The sense of life that created the American civilization was one that was marked by an absence of fear—fear of man the individual, the universe, and the immediate environment in which he planted his roots and forged an ever-evolving identity. The prototype of a human being created by the Founding Fathers was one that transcended the tribalism of European man and the birth-to-cradle role-identity that was his destiny. In fact, so magnanimous was the sense of life of the Founders, that they were the first in history to liberate the individual from his or her historicity. They created a civilization where persons could forget where they came from and where the aspiration for economic mobility took precedence over social status. Unlike European aristocrats who looked down upon those who had to work, work was a badge of honor and the new currency used to regulate the transactional and trader principle among human beings.

For the first time in his history, man—sanctioned by a political principle that defended his public identity—could exist in a state of *becoming*, a state where previous installments on his life could be modified, transfigured, or abandoned altogether depending on his ambitions, goals, and aspirational designs. It is true that European man had attempted this, but it was done in an individual, piecemeal fashion and separated from any ruling principle that promoted an aspirational identity he might have held.

The Founders were the first to give a secular application to the notion of transcendence. It was not escapism nor flight into mystical systems of *being* that disregarded the centrality of this earth. Profoundly in love with this earth and possessed of a sense that it belonged to man first and foremost, transcendence and becoming meant that man did not have to be determined then over-determined by historical roots and by the morally neutral accidents of birth. If he held onto them, he could do so lightly as a sociological and biographical detail of his life.

Becoming and transcendence in the new America meant that the individual could divest the social and inherited identity of its spirit of seriousness. An attribute of birth was not and could not be a definitive aspect of who a person was fundamentally. The social consequences of a political document that secured freedom for all and established inalienability of all rights and the equality of all persons were deeply emancipatory. It meant that the social and inherited attributes by which human beings were appraised were not only largely irrelevant, but in those cases where they were relevant, they were subject to innumerable contestations and contingent, provisional appraisals that were secondary considering what actions people took to support their existence. You were what you did, not fundamentally what you inherited. In the new America, with its limitless opportunities and unlimited freedom from arbitrary interference by the state, it was not impossible for a person to remake himself in his own image—not that of society, the tribe, or the family. The individual gave material meaning to autonomy and sovereignty over his life. For man to proudly declare that he was the owner of his life and that he could do with it as he pleased, and that such an utterance was guaranteed the support and protection of a Constitution, replete with a Bill of Rights, was so rare an occurrence in the history of mankind, we may, without hubris, say that the Founding Fathers created a First People—a chosen people not by a religious association with God. Rather, they became the new chosen people because, like a stylized work of art, the Founders had selectively recreated reality according to their strongest metaphysical value judgment guided by invariable laws of nature. The new human was the work of art they stylized and the new America the canvas upon which he or she would enact his or her life. We may say that this stylization was done by a resocialization of man spawned by the Constitution and the society it created.

The Founding Fathers were geniuses in another field of philosophy: aesthetics. The birth of a new political man with new moral sensibilities would, over a long period of time, create a social and political revolution—the creation of a cosmopolitan society open to all peoples, regardless of lineage and blood ties. It would be a nation that would gather foreigners and radical others into what came to be called a "melting pot," but which really meant an alliance among strangers around the core political values of the republic. It meant that each citizen could keep his ethnic and racial identity if he chose to, but that he would develop a thin political identity that all would share, regardless of concrete political commitments. They may disagree with each other in matters of public affairs, but they would defend the right of each to uphold his conception of the good for his life. The state would prioritize the right over the good, which meant that the state would remain silent on matters of personal choice, taste, and actions that constituted one's conception of the good—so long as they did not violate people's rights. However, it would champion principles of justice, fairness, and equality before the law.

In this endeavor, we see more than the sense of life of the Founders. We see their absolute commitment to the *right of the individual's property* in his own happiness, values, conscience, time, soul, mind, labor, body, and reason. This moral jurisdiction is an indivisible good from which one cannot be separated or alienated. To do this would result in the violation of the law of nature or reason in one's own person and would be a violation of the right to self-preservation.

We may surmise from the Founders' sense of life, some phenomenon—like *civic love*—was forged in the new America. We may now submit that the second instantiation of political eugenics created by the Founders was translating this civic love from a sentiment into an ethos, then into a sociopolitical reality. In the creation of a republic in which citizenship would, in the distant future, not be tied to tribal affiliation, the Founders created the first cosmopolitan country on earth. They did not create the cosmopolitan morality of the ancient Greek Cynics and Stoics, which was later developed by the Roman Stoics. The Founders accomplished a remarkable feat by making it possible for America to be opened to foreigners and strangers from all walks of life. It accepted the poor and huddled masses all over the world—those who were rejected and persecuted by their own societies and families—and offered them a chance to fulfil a universal end in the pursuit and achievement of happiness and their meaning and purpose in life.

It is into this ethical and political domain that the slave, the African indigene, would begin a long and protracted process of liberation—a body enslaved, but a soul tethered to a historical process and a sociopolitical and religious system in which he would eventually find moral freedom.

Slavery was horrific and incompatible with the grand narratives of the new republic. It violated the Christian moral eugenics that recognized the intrinsic moral worth of each person and the inviolable dignity each bore in his or her person.

America is the first country to insert itself in the world and offer itself up as a friend to humanity—a place where citizens everywhere can belong and play a role in suffusing the nation-state with an original assemblage of who one is.

It is the first, full-fledged cosmopolitan state for all the reasons advanced above and more—it inclines human beings not to search for their origins but, rather, their destiny. It is the first nation in history where—despite lip service to hyphenated identities that are purely symbolic—human beings have been driven to flee from their origins and remake themselves through a process of becoming a new specimen—oftentimes, a radically new person. The cosmopolitan moment here lies in the fact that the search for man's destiny demands an interaction with radically different others that forces him to revise the narrative construct on which his previous identity was predicated.

A spiritual transformation occurs in the act of migration and settling. The distancing of oneself from roots is an act of creating that which the individual was born tethered to: *genetic associative root connection.* America was the first country that incentivized the individual to prioritize the future over the past, to eschew nostalgia in favor of hope and aspiration, and, in so doing, to keep alive the pulsating energy that vitalizes a nation twenty-four hours per day, 365 days per year.

True, the African indigene was an involuntary migrant, one brought by force to America, but it is too late to alter that fact. It is into this domain, created by the Founders of the American republic, that he has developed a universal, moral personality and become part of the sovereign mass. Contemporary Afro-centrists who valorize some harkening back to an authentic African identity commit gross category mistakes. The African indigene did not hold an African identity—his was strictly tribal and local. They are lumping together a set of linguistically and tribally disparate groups of Africans who had different mores and protocols under a univocal rubric which they can use to meticulously organize and give moral coherence to their fabricated identities.

The shibboleths have spoken. Africa does not and cannot exist for black Americans today for the simple reason that the Africa from which today's ancestors were born and brought into slavery does not exist. Every black American living today has more in common with his or her fellow white compatriot than with the contemporary African on the continent. The Afro-centrist has lost his origins in Africa; his proper lineage and birthright belong here, in America. He had no authentic religion in Africa, save for variations on themes of primitive animism, fertility earth cults, ancestral worship, and a multiplicity of practices that, on retrospective examination, look like sorcery and witchcraft.

Physically enslaved, the slave was able to contemplate the horror of his condition, conceive of himself as a free agent, and therefore, acquire a degree of contempt for the institution of slavery. In this transformative passage during enslavement, the former indigene held a vestige of honor and dignity, which was possible because his soul was freed by the gift of a religious tradition that, though foisted on him, turned him from a natural creature into a moral personality. This very religion, Judeo-Christianity, often used as a justification for his enslaved condition, preached moral eugenics that revealed him equal to all men in the eyes of God, one possessed of intrinsic moral worth and inviolable dignity. It taught him that before Christ all were reborn and made anew and that none had a higher share in divinity or humanity than any other. It made him the beneficiary of a radical, spiritual, egalitarian belief system that sustained him during the worst period in American history and that would form the soul of the new African American. That soul, born in pain and suffering but freed by the proclamations of universal moral abolitionist systems of fraternity, brotherhood, and inalienability, would suffuse the landscape with its inimitable sound. It would become a constitutive part of America's very identity after centuries of deliberate efforts of exclusion.

In any contestation between objective reality and subjective viewpoints, reality is always the final arbiter: self-evident truths that are held and known to be true but denied and delayed out of expediency will eventually win the day.

THREE

Moral Eugenics Applied: The 1964 Civil Rights Act and The Radical Third Founding of America

We may locate the Third Founding of the United States in the 1964 Civil Rights Act and its various amendments, the 1965 Voting Rights Act, and other attendant pursuant articles and legal enfranchisements for blacks, including the Equal Employment Opportunity Act of 1972.

I place what I will later refer to as reparations for black Americans into the plethora of affirmative action programs that set aside preferential policies in education and employment for blacks and women.

The 1964 Civil Rights Act was as revolutionary as the founding of America and the Bill of Rights. Not only did it single-handedly right the wrongs of slavery and Jim Crow segregation, but in violating the property rights of US citizens (I shall say later on say why this could be reasonably justified), it was the most audacious act of cultural and moral eugenics ever leveled against the United States of America. It resulted in the broadest moral resocialization and social engineering program of white Americans in the history of this country. The concomitant moral eugenics was a form of moral paternalism and intrusion in the conscience of white Americans. It was an abrogation of freedom of conscience and the application of that conscience in concretized, material form.

The Civil Rights Act of 1964 enacted on July 2 of that year, was a landmark civil rights and labor law that outlawed discrimination based on race, color, religion, sex, national origin, and later, sexual orientation. It prohibits unequal application of voter registration requirements, racial segregation in all schools and public accommodations, and any employment discrimination. Under the Act, Congress asserted its authority to legislate under various parts of the Constitution, especially to regulate interstate commerce. It guaranteed all citizens equal protection under the laws under the Fourteenth Amendment and exercised its duty to protect voting rights under the Fifteenth Amendment.

The Equal Opportunity Employment Act of 1972, a federal law that amended Title VII of the Civil Rights Act of 1964, addressed employment discrimination against black Americans and other minorities. It empowered the Equal Employment Opportunity Commission to take legal action against individuals, employers, and labor unions that violated the employment provisions of the 1964 Act. The commission also required employers to make reasonable accommodation for the religious practices of employees.

Forthcoming shall be a full discussion of the 1964 Act in the form of affirmative action policies; but, for now, I will focus on the procedural and distributive form of justice achieved by the Act, as well as the cultural consequences that followed affecting not only the lives of black people but whites as well. The target of the 1964 Act was as much whites as it was blacks—and not just in the sense of mandating that whites cease egregious practices of discrimination against blacks, but, rather, that whites become entirely new types of persons by undergoing a moral makeover.

The moral revolution fought to free the slaves from bondage under the auspices and heroic efforts of President Lincoln was insufficient to achieve full freedom for blacks. The proper moral action would have been to free the slaves and educate them as full members of the state, assimilate them into mainstream society, and conjoin their personal sensibilities with those of the political values of the republic. They ought to have been admitted into the domain of the ethical and the pantheon of the human community. But the psychosis that is racism predicated on—a theme of biological collectivism which, in turn, uses race as means to achieve and maintain power—kept black Americans outside the realm of participatory citizenship, civic education, and, *a fortiori*, the historical process.

Through their own grit, tenacity, and creative agency, blacks, upon emancipation, were able to—in spite of efforts to exclude them from society—insert themselves in the historical process. During the most virulent forms of segregation and disenfranchisement, they came into their own and held an awareness of their intrinsic moral dignity, sovereignty, and autonomy, and fought for a *conception* of themselves as free individuals. That mainstream white society did not consistently contribute to their moral and cultural matriculation but, instead, created arbitrary and discriminatory laws to keep them on the margins of society was a practice of putative white supremacy, ugly bigotry, and pure racial hatred.

Blacks, though, were culturally and linguistically assimilated. Many were patriots, and during the period when whites were at their worst, they were at their best in developing their moral and intellectual capabilities.

The state had been the biggest manufacturer of systemic racism by creating laws that barred blacks from full entrance into mainstream society and had been a great socializer in the formation of the ethos, mores, norms, and values that shaped the sensibilities of whites. In short, it made it difficult for non-racist whites to be non-racist in their dealings with blacks. Homeowners and hoteliers were not free to sell or rent to whomever they chose regardless of race, and miscegenation laws prohibited interracial marriage. Conceptions of the good life were vastly limited for blacks based on their racial identities created not by private citizens but by the state. The establishment of racial taxonomies, of miscegenation laws, of redlining policies, and of discriminatory housing and school policies were all creations of the state—the biggest and most nefarious enemy of black Americans who had deputized and socialized ordinary American citizens into a cult of racist practices against their fellow citizens.

The 1964 Civil Rights Act was, therefore, no altruistic gift to black Americans, nor was it a repaid debt. The latter implies legitimate (or illegitimate) transactional exchanges between parties that call for payment to a creditor by one who had been temporarily accorded funds or some agreed-upon value by another party (the creditor). Debt is deferred payment.

The confiscation of freedom was a moral infraction against blacks' inalienable and inviolable right to bodily integrity and hereditary freedom. What they required was justice—the correction of a wrong done to them. The 1964 Civil Rights Act accomplished that. In granting blacks full equality before the law, the state reversed a metaphysical crime it had long been guilty of committing against the former slaves: failure to apply the principle of legal egalitarianism to one group of people for a morally neutral reason—their ascriptive racial identity. The latter was used to expel them from the domain that included those enjoying the hereditary rights of man. Egalitarianism can only be plausible in the legal sense—that is, all persons should be regarded as having equal moral worth, inalienable rights, and, therefore, treated equally before the law. That people are not equal in strength, beauty, intelligence, moral behavior, and so on ought to make no difference as to how they are treated by the law. We have seen how the Founders and advocates for black freedom, including Abraham Lincoln, pressed this principle.

The 1964 Act granted blacks full inclusion into the domain of the ethical by giving them identical status it had bestowed upon whites: they were now a protected class—protected from the arbitrary encroachments of others against the unassailability of their inalienable rights. In one sense, the 1964 Act was the great equalizer. It did not make anything special of blacks in its initial inception, although it did end up exceptionalizing them in order to remedy the egregious injustices of the past.

By recognizing blacks as equal citizens before the law, the 1964 Act proclaimed that, as far as the republic was concerned, blacks now had full access to the global commons—they fully belonged to America and, concomitantly, America belonged to them. By outlining how they could legally exercise their creative agency, many blacks, conscious of themselves as possessing moral freedom, intrinsic dignity, inviolable worth, and inalienable rights, knew that nothing could prevent them from suffusing the American landscape with an original assemblage of who they were by law.

They were no longer interpretable metaphors outside the historical process. They were contributors—as they had been since they were freed from slavery—to American civilization in education, entrepreneurship, medicine, sports, real estate, theology, and a myriad of other fields.

Blacks had forged an indelible identity and were exercising their agency in ways that were thoroughly American. Their endeavor was imprinted on the landscape as part of the national identity of the country. It would take a while before a majority of white Americans would recognize the legitimacy of their contributions as constitutive of the bourgeoning soul of America. The country was and remains, comparatively speaking, a new nation. The majority of blacks (if any) had no knowledge of ancestral African languages from which any semblance of their pre-American cultural identities could be linked. There did not seem to be large swaths who seemed interested in returning to a motherland they had long been separated from. America was home. America was destiny. America was the promised land. Holding a firm conception of themselves as a free people possessed of inviolable dignity with no less or greater share of humanity than their white counterparts, they followed the call of moral and political freedom to its logical terminus—a demand for equal standing before the law.

The 1964 Civil Rights Act would establish more than this, however. During the horrific violence visited upon blacks during the movement to end segregation, when millions of Americans saw German shepherds and fire hoses tuned against unarmed and non-responsive black people, as they saw elderly black men, women, and children pummeled in the streets by police wielding bloodied batons, something almost mystical happened that transformed the white imaginary in this country. The black body—passive, submissive, and broken—became a meditative site for universal suffering, white shame, guilt, moral horror, and revulsion. It became a moment for contrition, redemption, repentance, and deep introspection on the part of white Americans as to how they wished their nation to proceed as a republic. It could be divided and bifurcated along racial lines with a separately configured humanity for two distinct human types. Or, in keeping with the moral meaning of America and the original spirit of the nation's founding, it could involve a common humanity for all persons created in the image of one God who administered law equally to all and who did not favor any of his children more than others, based on any accidents ascribed to their births.

In the end, a nation, not without contention and protestations, passed a bill that made private racial discrimination illegal. As previously discussed, Title VII of the Civil Rights Act of 1964 and the Equal Employment Opportunity Act of 1972 became landmark pieces of legislation. The term *equal,* however, must be interpreted correctly as it applies to this legislation. It does not mean that every applicant or employee must be considered equal in ability or competency. Rather, it means that the law looks at all applicants or employees as equals who deserve fair treatment. Specifically, it requires that no applicant or employee may be rejected from employment or treated unfairly solely because of race, religion, color, national origin, or sex. The law requires that the most competent applicants be hired, and the most competent employees be promoted.

The law does not promise a job or a promotion. It is meant to level the playing field and make the rules the same for all applicants and employees. Equal employment opportunity programs include affirmative action as well as means for handling discrimination complaints. The law applies to everyone who is in a position to hire individuals.

By illegalizing private racism, it criminalized the applied judgment of private conscience when that conscience applied itself in the realm of private ownership in the public realm. The government basically proclaimed to entrepreneurs and business owners, "You cannot treat your business as a mere extension of your home or your living room. You cannot use your property—which is the material application of your reason conjoined with your personal labor which, in turn, is an expression of your abstract values made concrete—in a manner that discriminates against blacks."

The state's role here was two-fold in that it was not just about the legal emancipation of blacks from the stranglehold of centuries of white domination, but the moral rehabilitation of whites who had sullied their souls and those of their descendants by continuing the mores and enhancing the ethos associated with slavery. That such actions lead to putative rights denial was indisputable.

I submit that the 1964 Civil Rights Act was an act of moral eugenics, an enormous social engineering program made to reshape the moral sensibilities of whites. It was, on one hand from the perspective of morality, necessary. Simultaneously, I think it was enacted also for the redemption of the white soul of America. It was beyond making legal demands of whites. It, in the end, was didactic, invasive, and ended up functioning like a comprehensive, legislative, moral doctrine that partially determined one way people could not cultivate conceptions of the good lives for themselves. The state declared to whites: "Harbor racist beliefs in your mind as much as you like, but you'd better not materially organize a lived life around those racist principles. You cannot apply them in reality."

I say the 1964 Act was a form of moral eugenics not to be hyperbolic. Aside from violating property rights, the state was also deliberately and knowingly violating freedom of conscience. Let us be clear: freedom of conscience only has resonance and existential traction when its corollaries—the judgments of one's mind—can be applied here in reality. Not even in a bloated totalitarian state can conscience in the sense of secretly holding one's beliefs, convictions, and principles be denied. The right to conscience acquires conceptual validity and existential traction only when it pertains to application and action in the world. In barring racists from applying their racist conscience into concrete practice in the form of privately discriminating against blacks in their private establishments, the state contravened into the realm a sacred right of which citizens of any modern republic are the legatees—the right to freedom of one's conscience. If one is restricted from living by the dictates of one's conscience one is—whether they are right or wrong—paternalistically prevented from exercising one's deepest values and convictions.

The racist would say that in refusing to privately deal with a black person he is not violating that person's rights for the sole reason that such a person has no automatic right to the products of his labor. If he runs a restaurant, then food service is a service he provides for customers he wishes to serve, not an inalienable right others have to consume his food. Another human can have no right to the product of one's efforts that one has produced on behalf of one's life. One is in ownership of the material expression of one's mind and values applied to reality.

Yet, the 1964 Act and its subsequent amendments ruled that blacks and other minorities did have such a right. The state used it to communicate that one's racist conscience was so vile that it no longer had a place as a moral pollutant in the public sphere. The Act was meant to invite moral opprobrium and the concomitant emotions of shame and guilt. If one felt no shame and guilt, then it was further indication of one's moral bankruptcy. How could one arbitrarily discriminate against a fellow compatriot on a criterion—skin color—that had no connection to the moral character of that human being?

To be prejudiced, the architects of the moral eugenics and social engineering program suggested, was not only a form of moral slothfulness, but it was also to continue the practice of biological collectivism—that is, ascribing moral value and worth to someone's racial ascriptive identity and all those who share it. On that sole basis, one makes the psychotic assumption that those who did not share such an identity were not only devoid of some mystical, chemical predestination suffused with moral attributes, but that they lacked in-depth humanity and moral worth.

Racism was, for the first time, designed to make one sound like a village idiot, if not consciously, then by a slow process affixed to its practitioners by means of converting white racial pride from a mark of authentic American identity into one of a shameful social stigma.

The meaning of what it meant to be as an American was shifting. Black faces conjoined with white ones in a struggle for legal and economic equality were also rebranding the metaphysical identity of the nation itself. The major players who would be forced, by default, to partake in the rebranding would be whites. The nation was moving in a direction driven by its shameful past to traduce individuals for their racist actions—the twin moral opprobrium of racial domination and racial exclusion were being cast as atavistic and anathema to the new republic.

This is why I have called the passage of the 1964 Civil Rights Act the Third Founding of America. This legislation was a bold act of moral and political peroration. The principle of egalitarianism was being applied outside the sphere of mere legality. Whites may have worked for their property and indulged in rhetorical plinth to shore up the right that secured it; however, something transformational was taking place in the new America. Think about it this way—the nondiscriminatory clauses affixed to the Civil Rights Act protected government property from government appropriation but not from public access!

In other words, though services had to be paid for, *access* could never be denied. This made private property that was communally accessible by government decree a form of "social property." Much like children being forced to share their toys, property becomes communal in myriad ways. Before the formal instantiation of affirmative action, there was *affirmative access* to privately owned property. Eminent domain, which placed absolute control of private property outside the personal jurisdiction of individual property holders, was thought to be a nefarious breach in the founding principles of America. Now blacks held a default third property share in the private property of whites. If property, as classically conceived, is an extension of one's mind—the material application of the thinking one has done and, further, if one has to sustain one's life by one's efforts and the concrete result of those efforts—that means that one's sovereignty and autonomy are also superimposed upon and compromised by the actions of others. If the right to the pursuit of happiness is linked to the right to pursue property and dispose of it as one wishes, then blacks, backed by the state, were in the unique position of appropriating the moral happiness created by private individuals through their property creations.

Through its moral eugenics program, the state had inverted the principle of the right to property. The right to property is a right to action, *simpliciter,* not a right to an object. It is the right to pursue the efforts and actions that will result in the creation of or acquisition of property by earning it. The right to property does not guarantee that any person will earn property; it guarantees that one will own it if one earns it. One then earns the right to keep, use, and dispose of those material values which led to the procurement of property.

The eugenic moment of the Civil Rights Act is expressed in the premise: human rights supersede property rights. Gone were the days for white property owners when they could claim to use their lawfully-gained black labor as a means to further their ends and see their lives as inextricably tied to their property as an end in itself. Blacks were granted permission to appropriate white property for personal—albeit paid—consumption, to modify white conceptions of personal happiness and conceptions of the good that informed it. We may call this moral socialism.

THE MORAL RESOCIALIZATION OF AMERICANS

As visionary, progressive architects build public parks, habitats, offices, and public passage in ways that invite greater social contact to encourage collective or creative social intercourse among citizens rather than, say, solitary, individualistic pursuits, so the moral eugenics of the new America were redesigning a conception about how the public sphere ought to look. The new America (imperfect as the instantiation of the vision was, given continued racial discrimination) would not just be an integrated one. There is no faster way to integrate a society than through fiscal models. One side of the Civil Rights Act was anointed with holy justice.

The other was stamped with the imprimatur of enforced convivality, which was a veneer behind which lay laws that explicitly mandated the terms of employment between the races and the rules of engagement between whites and blacks in white-owned businesses. Personal property had become the equivalent of public utility companies. To take advantage of the exit clause that all liberal societies allow for dissatisfied citizens who have quarrel with the social contract was to risk bankruptcy.

It did not matter that many whites were not signatories to the new social compact that was replacing the old system that had been responsible for the enslavement and exclusion of blacks from mainstream society. They ratified it by their mere presence in the society.

One could say that the Civil Rights Act was a morally stupendous act of legal and moral freedom for blacks, an encroachment on the agency, conception of the good life, and freedom of whites who were being conscripted into a new Great Society where their outlaw sensibilities were being targeted and criminalized—at least by public decree. No public apology was necessary on the part of whites for their personal treatment of blacks. Adherence to the clauses of the Civil Rights Act and subsequent amendments positioned one as a supplicant and observant to and of the new law. Abidance was sufficient to absolve one of any personal damage they might have inflicted on any particular black person. The law itself, and its matriculation through society, became wholesale, as opposed to retail ways of achieving moral redemption, contrition, repentance, and atonement for inflicting past wrongs.

Stealth is how cultural eugenics wields itself in the public imaginary. There is a systematicity and efficiency to it that spares individuals overt embarrassment and humiliation. It imprints its imprimatur in the name of justice and objectivity with malice towards none. For though one could say the social engineering program that was part of the 1964 Civil Rights Act could have been humiliating for many whites, an argument could be made otherwise. All whites had to do was shield themselves behind the abstract nature of the law to which all were subjected. If they were so inclined, they could even have complained bitterly about how they found the law to be unjust, which many did. Some even resorted to being conscientious objectors.

When I speak about the new moral eugenics, it is important to bear in mind that it is inextricably linked to property rights, which are taken to be the basis and foundation for all other rights in our republic, including the right to life. To change the moral DNA of a nation and its citizens, it is not regarded as sufficient to engage in endless missionary sermonizing in churches or in the educational system about the equal, moral value of blacks; the social engineering of the transformative nature of the 1964 Civil Rights Act was not fought on the level of moral suasion—although civil rights leaders such as Dr. Martin Luther King did engage in that enterprise.

Instead, on a fundamental level, the sweeping change of the nation's racialist DNA would be effected and transmuted through property rights. It would involve a contestation of two competing conceptions of the right to life vying against each other—those of the unearned (blacks making a claim of a right to an object) superseding those of the producers (white business owners and employers). The latter group would yield to the demands of the former by law. In this act of continued supplication, a new understanding of human rights would take precedence over property rights. Whites were being morally retrained and rehabituated into a domain of new civic virtues.

As much as it was a legal document granting blacks equal standing before the law, it was also a new form of virtue theory directed at whites. To coerce a person into having a different relationship to his property, to how he fashions and organizes his life around his personal property, and, just as importantly, to leave him no choice but have him aver in one crucial area which he has always taken for granted—the public sphere, which became universally public—involved a monumental attitudinal shift. It was not a public sphere for the white population, but a universal and cosmopolitan sphere to which all had equal access and within which all would matriculate and continue their journey as human beings. Whites were not just giving up full jurisdiction over their property; they were relinquishing control of the global commons over which they had reigned as the normative and *de facto* beneficiaries. Beaches, public libraries, schools, parks, and streets—you name it—had been the domains in which an illusory white American and homogenous identity had been curated, succored, and cultivated. Forced integration in the social domains was one thing. In the private realm of property, it struck many whites as a second unconstitutional application of eminent domain—black settlers descending on white property without the permission of its owners.

For a significant number of whites, it was regarded as reverse occupation. As whites had occupied the bodies, expropriated the agency of blacks, and denied them property rights for centuries, so the Civil Rights Act was allowing them a quasi "paid squatters rights." *We are free to sit at your lunch counters, entertain ourselves in your movie theaters, define ourselves in your employment establishments, and invert the moral meaning of production and of capitalism: the right of human beings to trade and deal with whomever they desire based on mutual cooperative consent, each giving value for value.*

Such was the expropriative method of the Janus-faced nature the Civil Rights Act. It compromised the autonomy of the businessman, deprived him of jurisdictional independence over his property and, therefore, his life, liberty, and pursuit of happiness.

I submit that the 1964 Civil Rights Act was not just about procedural distributive justice. It was also a punitive and retributive document—as penal and discriminatory against a white person and his property as had never been seen before non-propertied white males had been granted the right to vote. Some would say these punitive measures scaled back the white individual's creative ability, ambitiousness, self-assertiveness, and his unlimited capacity to reshape the public domain and the earth itself in the image of his values.

"And so what?" comes the rejoinder. Given the horrific history of enslavement, of racial segregation, of white domination over blacks, and of the arbitrary creation of laws to keep blacks from accessing the social goods required to flourish on the massive scale permitted to whites, was the moral eugenics of the 1964 Civil Rights Act an egregious assault against white people and, if so, was it justifiable?

My answer is contentious.

Given the state's role in the creation of racial taxonomies that were used to justify white domination of blacks, the creation of discriminatory laws including miscegenation laws, discriminatory zoning laws in housing, education, prohibiting blacks from voting, and the myriad ways in which blacks were cast as second class citizens long after being ensconced in the historical process, we may conclude one thing—the state played a large role in manufacturing racists and was the enemy of blacks in several cases. They punished non-racist whites for not being racists.

Consider a non-racist hotelier who decided he would allow blacks to enter the front lobby of his hotel, rent large rooms to those who could afford them, and integrate them into the lavish dining areas reserved for whites only. Or the white woman who in the state of Virginia circa 1935 decided she wanted to marry the black schoolteacher with whom she fell in love. We could create myriad examples, but I assume our readers are familiar with sufficient history of this country's racist past to realize the dire consequences whites would face before the law for simply not adhering to racial protocols, to say nothing of the deadly consequences for blacks. Whites would have faced legal and social repercussions for not being racists, for not adhering to racist mores and norms of the society that engendered their socialization.

To what extent was freedom of association and freedom of conscience possible for whites in their relation to blacks before the Civil Rights movement? Could a white woman decide that she wanted to take her black girlfriends to her favorite restaurant or coffee shop? Could a businessman whose moral conscience decried racism in Mississippi in 1947 have brought in a black woman as head of human resources to oversee an all-white band of employees in his bank? Could he have done this if this black woman were the intellectual superior to all his white employees? No—the racial narratives of his era would not have permitted this type of cognitive appraisal performed by a black woman in the deep South or anywhere else in America.

It was not only the laws created in the United States Congress that discriminated against blacks that created racists in America. Equally problematic was the manner in which the state turned whites into racists by creating a political, legal, and environmental milieu that not only made it almost impossible to be conscientious objectors to the racist status quo, but created harmful, punitive measures against them had they ratified their conscience by exercising it in the form of applied non-racist actions.

Whites, in many instances, were as much the victims of immoral, racist machinations by the state as were blacks. They had their interior lives hijacked and sullied by state-sponsored discriminatory mandates and the concomitant ethos that emerged from them. Still, others voluntarily supported lynching and other evil actions against blacks, knowing with full forethought of malice that they were heinous acts. They failed to prosecute the perpetrators not because they were victims, but because they themselves were complicit with the state in the creation of the very toxic ethos others were exposed to.

In short, the state colluded with white citizens in promoting an ideology of white racial superiority—official white supremacy. Prior to the civil rights movement, it was socially accepted for whites to openly proclaim their belief in white racial superiority. In fact, both a *de jure* and *de facto* ideology of white supremacy was the norm up until the explicit passage of 1964 Civil Rights Act and the 1965 Voting Rights Act. I maintain that even post-1964, *de jure* white supremacy was a prevailing ethos in much of the United States for the simple reason that miscegenation laws remained on the books. It was not until *Loving v. Virginia*, 388 U.S. 1 (1967), a landmark civil rights decision of the Supreme Court in which it ruled that laws banning interracial marriage violated the Equal Protection and Due Process Clauses of the Fourteenth Amendment, that miscegenation laws—among the evilest of laws that could ever exist in a free society—were struck down in many states.

Marriage is neither a moral right nor a universal more. It is a derivative of the right to our personalities and is secured by the right of autonomy and self-ownership. Self-ownership is the means for securing the right to preservation, which, in turn, secures the right to life. Marriage is one of the most formal ways in which the highest values one holds are ratified by the state—friendship, love, bonds of affection, family, commitment, and oaths of loyalty and fidelity.

Given the centrality of valued persons in our lives, and the psychological need to have them esteemed in the public sphere, we understand marriage as, among other things, the insignia of public approval of the choices made by two people. We make sacred the union of such people by granting unto it the juridical imprimatur of the state. Marriage is beyond mere legality; it is taken to be the nucleus in which regeneration, social validation, and affirmation take place.

Those who would deprive interracial couples this derivative right are those who would exclude them from being formal co-constructors of the very society of which they are a part and would decouple them from the highest value they hold that, on several accounts, is a constitutive feature of their personal and moral identities.

The legalization of interracial marriage, the granting of suffrage to women, and the abolition of slavery are all emancipatory gestures on the part of human beings to have their lives thematically linked to the political morality of the state. The right to vote, the right not to be enslaved, and the freedom to form unions of love in marriage are not radical acts of difference. They are actions that, in stretching the constitutional mettle of a liberal union, ensure the existence of a just state, one that promises each the freedom to pursue his or her God-given right to life, liberty, and the pursuit of happiness.

We cannot get along with such persons who would prohibit interracial marriage because, among other things, they simply refuse to recognize the centrality of a basic human emotion between human beings—love. The failure to grant recognition to this emotion between two people renders them invisible. Invisibility before others is not a tenable state of affairs. To get along with such persons is to collude in the nonrecognition of oneself and the symbolic and legal destruction of one's highest value. Racial superiority is promoted through laws that prohibit marriage among members of so-called different racial groups on the premise that intermarriage, when applied to a group, violated customary practices that rested on a logic of contagion and contamination.

This was the worst form of social and biological collectivism propagated by the state and the milieu into which human beings were socialized and forced to conduct their moral lives, regardless of whether one was black or white.

Forget slavery—it would take miscegenation laws alone and the logic of those laws taken to their absolute conclusion to establish an official ideology of white supremacy in this country. Fortunately, that official ideology does not exist today, which speaks to the magnificent moral nature of the United States and its capacity for evolution and progress.

Nevertheless, in an ideal, just society that includes free blacks, all that the state is required to do is to leave them alone and create no legal barriers to obstruct them in their efforts in preserving their lives and their life plans. Since it is only the state that has a coercive monopoly on the use of force and the creation of laws, it is only the state that can legally enact measures to prevent blacks from life, liberty, and the pursuit of happiness. Private citizens who have discriminatory privileges do not have the power to legally enforce measures that arbitrarily single out blacks for legal discrimination based on morally irrelevant, neutral, morphological markers like skin color and ethnic identity.

From the time of their importation into America, the problem blacks faced was not one of becoming integrated into American society; rather, it was one of forced exclusion, which they overcame with their moral heroism, applied creative agency, grit, tenacity, resilience, perseverance, dignity, honor, and a firm commitment to the idea that race would not be determinant of their destiny, even at times when race played a significant role in shaping significant outcomes in their lives.

I have stated that the 1964 Civil Rights Act constituted a breach of private property and that it was a grand moral eugenics program that attempted to rehabilitate whites and make them into non-racists. The ethical question remains—was the breach in property rights justified? Was the social engineering fostered by the Civil Right Act a proper moral undertaking on the part of the state?

While remaining committed to the principle of free will and a philosophy of individualism, I submit that the original and contemporary enemy of black people is the state rather than the average white person.

When the state conjoins itself to individuals' moral conscience, and the latter performs in a manner that eviscerates blacks of their dignity and inalienable rights, when the consequences of the actions of the state against blacks backed by its surrogates—the deputized stand-in for white supremacy and dominion over blacks in the person of citizens—become such a ghastly and evil phenomenon, then the state, in recognition of the incalculable damage done to human life and flourishing, should properly criminalize racism when expressed in the public sphere. Private citizens did not codify and ratify the process by which human beings were maintained in vassalage and domination by diktat and decree.

A state that creates race laws and hijacks the moral conscience of its citizens and incentivizes them to be racists by the ethos, protocols, norms, and mores ratified formally cannot remove legal barriers and adopt a laid-back attitude to the racial and racist framework it created. The state has to adopt an activist role in rehumanizing vast swaths of human beings that it made into psychotic and irrational racists into moral creatures.

This activist role was achieved by state intrusion into the sphere of property ownership by white individuals. Property rights are not absolute; they are contextual. Blacks paid taxes to the state that then used their tax dollars in several cases to grant special contracts, subsides, and licensing to private contractors and business owners which failed to employ them. Many white-owned businesses were granted tax breaks and credits not afforded to black-owned businesses.

The federal government's investment in the Central Pacific Railroad development was a huge collusion between government and private enterprise. In the final analysis, the federal government made more money from land sales (all those sections near the right of way became very valuable) than it provided in subsidies. In fact, one of the provisions was that federal officials and military troops would travel for free on the transcontinental railroad; the federal government "cost avoidance" in free travel for its military more than paid for the railroad subsidy. From a taxpayer standpoint, it was a great investment! But was it for blacks?

What one has to admit—from a close and unbiased look at American history, from the subsidizing of the California railroad to special privileges granted to whites only—is that when the state colludes with whites to use their property to dehumanize blacks brought into the historical realm and in the realm of indivisible inalienability it is not sufficient to remove the barriers and leave the ethos, stereotypes, and prejudicial attitudes in place. Those prejudices and that collective ethos will simply be transmuted into other systems of racial discrimination backed by the state.

The full remittance of freedom requires a rewriting of the social status quo. Removal of a tumor from a body that had drained it of its nutrients and capacity to generate immune-building blood cells would not be sufficient for the proper functions of the body. Replacement and restorative therapy would be required to rebuild a wholesome body. The history of state discrimination against blacks and its enlistment of white conscripts to mainstream and normalize its policies of white supremacy resulted in the massive corruption in the humanity of all Americans citizens—especially white Americans. Private citizens can self-identity, but they cannot legislate into law the identities of others upon whom discriminatory actions are committed.

The state's racist policies were a cancerous blight against the noble ideals on which America was founded. Given, therefore, the various intrusions into the private lives of people, such as requiring marriage certificates to prevent members of certain groups from marrying others, the state has historically created a social reality predicated on evil, irrationality, prejudice, white supremacy, and systemic diminution of black agency.

Given the system of affirmative action for white business owners in the form of subsidies, patents, and government-backed, guaranteed loans in the railroad industry, farming, and banking, to name a few, financed by the extracted tax dollars from black and white citizens alike, for any such discrimination to have occurred against the very group of citizens (blacks) whose tax dollars were used to financially buttress or augment white businesses is an egregious wrong. Any person implicated in using property in state-backed racial discrimination could not, on behalf of their owners, claim property rights to be an unassailable non-contextual right.

I have made the case that the *moral eugenics* and what I have termed *moral socialism* on white Americans was a justifiable, albeit tragic ameliorative move on the part of the state to radically retransform what it had created from its inception. By accepting slavery into its founding, by creating a parallel society between blacks and whites, the state had manufactured—going as far back as the dissenting voices of the seventeenth-century Quakers and evangelical Christians who interpreted biblical equality as forbidding the ownership of men by others and thus saw slavery as both a political and moral evil—a toxic environment that harmed the moral lives of all its citizens.

Each white child born into the republic was reared on a diet of white supremacy and black inferiority. He or she was not told that blacks were their moral equals and that one day it would be just fine to marry a black person. To this extent, an egregious moral harm was done to whites. In being the bully aggressor in the violation of the individual rights of its citizens—especially blacks—the state created a political, legal, and social environment in which racism against blacks was not only acceptable but normatively expected.

Thus rests my defense for the moral eugenics dimensions of the 1964 Civil Rights Act and the far-reaching effects of its social engineering agenda.

The wrong was righted. If there was a debt to be repaid, it was repaid. Many white Americans emerged as better moral individuals who came to see, often through heavy-handed legal coercion, the psychosis on which racism rests. The moral eugenics of the whole civil rights movement effected a direct change in the disposition of the cognitive outlook of the average white American citizen.

But was that enough?

THE GREAT SOCIETY PROGRAMS OF 1960s AND THE GENESIS OF BLACK REPARATIONS THROUGH WELFARE

The arc of our journey into the question of what white Americans owe black people will find some semblance of completion in an answer to the question: Did black Americans emerge better off after the passage of the 1964 Civil Right Act and the Great Society programs launched by President Lyndon Johnson's administration?

This is a hotly debated topic, and I don't intend to rehash the minutiae of details that are now old hat. But the fundamental elements of Johnson's war on poverty and his Great Society programs and the ways in which they, arguably, contributed to the breakdown of the black family, increased crime rates in the black communities, high incarceration rates among black men, an astronomical increase in black on black murders, a more than doubling of black children born of out wedlock that correlated with poverty and single parent households, and above all, the appalling decline in black academic performance in public schools in historically black universities and in the nation's colleges, must all be noted and reckoned with.

In 2016, 965 people were shot by cops in the entire United States. Four percent of them were white cops shooting unarmed blacks. In 2011, twenty-one people were shot and killed by cops in Chicago. In 2015, there were seven. In Chicago, (which is about one-third white, one-third black, and one-third Hispanic) 70 percent of homicides during any given year, are black on black crimes. This amounts to about forty per month and almost 500 the previous year.

From 1890–1900, a black person was more likely to be born in a nuclear family than a white kid. At the height of segregation in America, 22 percent of blacks were married and had children in two parent households. According to the *Statistical Abstract of the United States*, in 1963, 72 percent of black families were married and living together. By 2017, however, that data was reversed—only 27 percent of black households were married. In comparison, the white population went from 89 percent married in 1963, down to 51 percent in 2017, a 39 percent decrease. Today, 73 percent of black children are born out of marriage with the vast majority born into poverty. According to *The Independent*, an independent non-partisan think tank publication of the Brookings Institution:

> "Children raised by single mothers are more likely to fare worse on a number of dimensions, including their social achievement, their social and emotional development, their health, and their success in the labor market. They are at a greater risk of parental abuse and neglect (especially from live-in boyfriends who are not their

biological father), more likely to become teen parents and less likely to graduate from high school or college."

The extant literature on the ways that the dispensation of welfare checks and Johnson's war on poverty hampered black agency is gargantuan. Arguments have been made that his welfare programs have disincentivized black men from providing for their families and that it married women to the state and incentivized them to have more children. The programs have been attributed to the breakdown of the black family, which, in turn, has led to fatherless households and an epidemic of directionless black youth who have turned to a life of crime and gang warfare as a substitute.

Critics of Johnson's programs have offered counter arguments by claiming that the link between crime and poverty vis-à-vis blacks is an invention. They point to the relatively low crime rates in black communities, including Harlem, before the 1960s and the late advancement of the civil rights movement.

According to Wikipedia, the "war on poverty" is as follows:

> [This] is the unofficial name for legislation first introduced by United States President B. Lyndon Johnson during his State of the Union address on January 8, 1964. This legislation was proposed by Johnson in response to a national poverty rate of around 19 percent. The speech led the United States Congress to pass the Economic Opportunity Act and established the Office of Economic Opportunity (OEO) to administer the local application of federal funds

targeted against poverty. The forty programs established by the act were collectively aimed at eliminating poverty by improving living conditions for residents of low-income neighborhoods and by helping the poor access economic opportunities long denied them.

As a part of the Great Society, Johnson believed in expanding the federal government's roles in education and health care as poverty reduction. These policies can also be seen as a continuation of Franklin D. Roosevelt's New Deal, which ran from 1933 to 1937, and Roosevelt's Four Freedoms of 1941. Johnson stated, "Our aim is not only to relieve the symptom of poverty, but to cure it and, above all, to prevent it."

The legacy of the war on poverty policy initiative remains in the continued existence of such federal government programs as Head Start, Volunteers in Service to America (VISTA), TRIO, and Job Corps.

Deregulation, growing criticism of the welfare state, and an ideological shift to reducing federal aid to impoverished people in the 1980s and 1990s culminated in the Personal Responsibility and Work Opportunity Act, which President Bill Clinton claimed "ended welfare as we know it."

But before welfare ended, the Great Society program had specifically targeted black families and the recipients of tax dollars from the middle- and high-income classes. Millions of government checks were printed and mailed and cashed. In the words of Stanford economist Martin Anderson, "The most ambitious attempt to redistribute income ever undertaken in the United States had begun."

I submit that the war on poverty and the Great Society programs aimed largely at blacks were *the* beginning of formal reparations. The social welfare programs of the 1960s resulted in the government displacing black fathers as bread winners and made work less attractive. Before Lyndon Johnson's war on poverty, it is true that New York and several other states had already begun expanding their own social welfare programs.

Johnson, I believe, knew that he was embarking on an unacknowledged reparative program that could only be justified in the registers of a national program for all poor people, but whose beneficiaries would be mainly black.

In 1965 in his commencement address at Howard University, "To Fulfill These Rights," Johnson unveiled, in a thinly disguised way, the commencement of his comprehensive social affirmative action for blacks. Like the moral eugenics and social engineering agenda unleashed by the 1964 Civil Rights Act, the war on poverty and Great Society programs were not just a disguised form of reparations for black Americans—it was the beginning of the expropriation of their moral, creative, and existential agency. It would result in the emasculation of black men and the psychological dependence of black women on the state as a surrogate husband—a loyal and faithful sugar daddy that came with a guaranteed paycheck each month and more money if she delivered another baby by a biological baby daddy who needn't stay around for the birth of his child.

But what did Johnson say that proves that he had embarked not just on a wealth redistribution program the likes of which the country had never seen, but also reparations for slavery and its aftermath? He declared in his speech at Howard University:

> "The voting rights bill will be the latest and, among the most important, in a long series of victories. But this victory—as Winston Churchill said of another triumph for freedom—'is not the end. It is not even the beginning of the end. But it is, perhaps, the end of the beginning.'
>
> That beginning is freedom; and the barriers to that freedom are tumbling down. Freedom is the right to share, share fully and equally, in American society—to vote, to hold a job, to enter a public place, to go to school. It is the right to be treated in every part of our national life as a person equal in dignity and promises to all others.
>
> But freedom is not enough. You do not wipe away the scars of centuries by saying: Now you are free to go where you want, and to do as you desire, and choose the leaders you please.
>
> You do not take a person who, for years, has been hobbled by chains and liberate him, bring him up to the starting line of a race and then

say, 'you are free to compete with all the others,' and still justly believe that you have been completely fair.

Thus, it is not enough just to open the gates of opportunity. All our citizens must have the ability to walk through those gates.

This is the next and the more profound battle for civil rights. We seek not just freedom but opportunity. We seek not just legal equity but human ability, not just human equality as a right and a theory but equality as a fact and equality as a result.

For the task is to give 20 million Negroes the same chance as every other American to learn and grow, to work and share in society, to develop their abilities—physical, mental, and spiritual, and to pursue their individual happiness.

To this end equal opportunity is essential, but not enough, not enough…."

To uphold a moral eugenics program that reformulated a poisoned social milieu still leaves free the moral agency of blacks to navigate their way in that environment without becoming economic wards of the state and an economic supplicant.

The 1964 Civil Rights Act established political egalitarianism, which is an unassailable right and moral good. All persons deserve to be treated equally in the eyes of the law because discrimination on the basis of morally neutral, arbitrary characteristics, such as skin pigmentation, the country of national origin, or religious affiliation and gender while affording the same right to persons who share contrasting attributes that are as equally morally neutral, is just categorically wrong.

But Johnson was attempting a feat more audacious than that. He was trying to revert the laws of identity and causality by introducing metaphysical egalitarianism—the idea that all men are born or acquire talents, skills, and capabilities of equal proportion in intelligence, strength, discipline, perseverance, frugality, temperance, frugality, tenacity, exercise of our rational faculty, wisdom, moral sensibility, and a plethora of other dispositions that determine outcomes. Or he may have been attempting to do something worse—if such talents, capabilities, and dispositions were not equally allocated among the races and individuals, then the state would need to artificially interfere and ensure that equality of outcomes and results proceeded equality of opportunity. In other words, he was mandating equal results from unequal causes or equal rewards for unequal performance.

Before moving on further to critique this notion and show how it had a devastating effect on the agency of black individuals and resulted in the emasculation of black men in general and before explaining why metaphysical egalitarianism runs contrary to human nature and natural law and is also a violation of the principle on which America was founded (political equality and not economic equality), I want to explain why even *equality of opportunity* is a politically untenable goal in a free society.

Equality of opportunity sounds like a beautiful thing to most people and, in an ideal utopia in which all persons were blessed with equal abilities and exercised the choices and judgments in a consistently rational and productive manner, one could imagine such an ideal being approximated. But what is an opportunity?

An opportunity is a set of circumstances that makes it possible to do something and achieve a goal. Equality of opportunity rests on trying to equalize initial chances of success. But exactly how does one do this without trespassing on the rights of others? A single mother who works three jobs to send her two children to private school—both of whom work very hard and graduate with honors—provides them with better opportunities to attend Ivy League colleges, as opposed to the parent who sends his child to a mediocre public school. The single mother's children who graduate from Wharton business school and Harvard Law School will have more employment opportunities than Mary Joe, whose children opted not to go to college or even trade school, but who occasionally apply for jobs for which they are not remotely qualified. After hours of tedious work, the mother who reads to her child every night before she falls asleep and engenders a passion for books in her young daughter, who later goes on to become a successful book editor, has put more effort into educating that child than a parent for whom reading before bedtime seems pointless.

Are black NBA players who dominate in basketball to be penalized because they have more opportunities for playing the sport than Asian men?

Freedom of equality of rights is what ought to be prized in a free society and the freedom to take advantage of opportunities as they avail themselves to us ought to be our goal.

Freedom of opportunity is predicated on the notion that circumstances that are often the result of value-generated actions of others should be controlled by the state. This is a recipe for totalitarianism. Even under a totalitarian state, it is empirically untenable. One cannot control the multiplicity of variables generated from human creative agency that produce opportunities for oneself and others.

Belief in equality of opportunity is a form of magical thinking because its advocates purport to master the existence of phenomena that do not yet exist. Opportunities arise as human beings are free to pursue their values and exercise efforts on behalf of their lives. Values result from attributes persons possess that cannot be redistributed. What the advocates of both equality of opportunity and result wish to do is to deprive persons the result of the consequences of their actions. The attempt to redistribute the products of a person's values indiscriminately is a form of appropriation that is impossible and irrational, and, therefore, unethical.

There is no zero-sum game here. Opportunities lead to actions, avenues, and venues for others to properly take advantage of and benefit from. But freedom, rather than abstract legislation mandating equal results, is what makes equality even possible.

Equality of results relies less on magical thinking than equality of opportunity. Appropriators take a country's aggregate of wealth that exists as a single conceptual unit and speak as if it were national wealth that was meant to be distributed. Wealth is not a cake that belongs to a nation; it is the concrete manifestation of the abstract values that humans hold applied here on earth. It belongs to those individuals who created it and ought not be seized by society.

The appropriators fail to realize that economic inequality is inevitable, as men are not born equal, and they also avoid the fact that the United States was founded not upon the principle of economic equality but political equality. Wealth that is privately built by individual effort is not created on the assumption that the creator of that wealth will end up with an equal share of it—in fact, quite the opposite. As Yaron Brook and Don Watkins point out in their book, *Equal is Unfair*, if I plant ten apple trees on an island, and Jack plants five, one cannot say I have grabbed a bigger part of the island's apple pie, so to speak. I have created more wealth than Jack, and I have left him no worse off. It would be absurd to say that I have stolen 50 percent of the island's wealth. If Jack made a choice not to plant extra trees, having spent his time relaxing under a coconut tree instead, there is no reason why I should be penalized for the extra initiative I have taken in planting the extra apple trees and cultivating them.

Black Americans, in participating in the massive welfare reparations programs of the 1960s, were complicit in the stigmatization that came to be associated with the extortion from wealthier Americans who paid for their financial upkeep. Blacks sold out their autonomy, sovereignty, and pride for entitlements they were told they deserved. They voluntarily evicted themselves from that competitive and venturesome realm in which the American Dream is achieved. The American Dream, however, was never achieved through a government handout.

Blacks are now part of the sovereign mass. The achievement of that status prior to the 1964 Civil Rights Act was not theirs to claim and enjoy entirely. Like all persons, who through legislative and judicial processes are admitted into the judicial and ethical pantheon, they must face a harsh truth. There will be inequities, inequalities, and disparities. But life itself is not predicated on equality because, again, we are all not equal. In fact, disparity and inequality are the norm. What must be secured are the foundations of freedom, liberty, and equality of rights. The civil rights movement was galvanized by blacks offering their victimized bodies as universal sites of suffering and as objects worthy of meditation and ethical contemplation. Their bruised and battered bodies served as ethical reminders that violation of bodily integrity and the ugliness of applied racism should invite moral shame into the heart of every racist.

Once the state recognized blacks, however, as part of the sovereign mass, they did not disappear into racial anonymity. They were now something special. They were certified moral icons stamped with a victim status—one that had the imprimatur of permanent innocence and the insignia of sainthood. To retain that status, they sacrificed their dignity and became economic supplicants of the state.

The cult of economic dependency has now lasted for over fifty-six years. It has drained many in the black community of their creative agency, eviscerated them of their dignity, turned them into pitiable mendicants and, above all, sent the life-denying message that one's fate and destiny lie outside one's own hands, that one is not responsible for oneself, and that white Americans are responsible for one's salvation. It sent the message that misfortune represents a legitimate mortgage on the purse strings of others.

For many black Americans who participated in the Great Society welfare reparations program, supplication became a form of strategic self-presentation where one presented their incompetence, weakness, and helplessness. The purpose of appearing helpless is to showcase one's dependence on others to procure help or sympathy. One does not merely need to pretend to be dependent—one must manufacture inadequacies to legitimize dependency and the attendant chronic relief that alleviates the suffering which produces it.

Blacks who are socialized to believe white Americans owe them anything other than respect for their individual rights are being taught to behave like slothful panhandlers who exaggerate destitution to exploit the sympathies of whites in order to procure more of their wealth. Supplicants exploit their weakness by throwing themselves at the mercy of others, thereby canceling out the possibility of achieving any form of moral equality with their benefactors.

Whites, I believe, suffer not only guilt but also embarrassment at the spectacle of repeated black failure and destitution. Many white individuals, therefore, *pretend* to become moral masochists—they believe that only by extending black suffering into an indefinite future whose amelioration depends on their beneficence can they repent, atone for, and achieve redemption for unnamed harm they or their ancestors have caused blacks. By engaging in this quasi-medieval morality play, many white people gain their moral and cosmic significance in the world. The end of the play culminates in a desire to see black people suffer forever so that they can retain their salvific identity and cosmic significance. This makes those white individuals into *moral sadists*. We may justifiably say, therefore, that at the heart of charity lies a great deal of moral sadism.

The black supplicant must chronically see the world as a place in which no efficacious action is possible, at least none of the sort that could ameliorate or emancipate him from his economically strained position. To live in a world in which one believes that efficacious actions cannot influence choices but can affect one's destiny is to exist in a monstrously intolerable state. This mode of existence leads to chronic anxiety and depression among such individuals.

Addiction to the financial beneficence of others becomes their only escape route.; the supplicant, therefore, must place his salvation solely in the hands of another. But actions are born out of reflection, deliberation, rational reflection, judgment, and choices. Often, the emancipatory action on which the supplicant is dependent is forged in the aspirational identity of the one who claims himself as the financial and, *inter alia*, moral redeemer.

Dependent blacks will remain second class citizens if they submit to an agreeable suppliance on the terms of the welfare state.

Economic supplication and its logical corollary—an inverted moral identity—based on the view of oneself as a distinct non-value, breeds a pervasive sense of self-inferiority and self-abnegation since it takes traits such as despondency, weakness, helplessness, victimization, and slothfulness as constitutive features of one's identity. They oversaturate the self to such an extent that the aspirational component of "the who one is" gets canceled. If one is alienated from their creative and transcendent nature and fed a philosophy that sees the absence of white relief as tragic, then the fate of the black individual is hermetically sealed in a racially bigoted world. If the black individual ventures out to make it on his own, he will be physically lost. The navigational reaches of his soul that direct him through life will be adrift.

The putative, self-defeating policies of the 1960s that allocated additional funds to unmarried women for each child they gave birth to conceal questions very few people want to broach but that must be asked—are we responsible for the procreative choices that others make? Should those procreative choices, however irresponsible, be passed off to society as a whole? Do we have a constitutional right to have children we cannot afford to maintain? Is it a form of neglect to bring more children into the world than you can afford to support? When you have children, is it fair to expect your neighbors to bear in the financial responsibility of raising them when they may have decided not to have any or to have just one, two, or just the exact number their budget can afford over the course of a lifetime? By what moral right would anyone dare tell you, who have sacrificed and planned your lives carefully and are already in debt and sending your children to school, that by his or her racial identity, that you—regardless of your race—have a responsibility to finance his or her college education?

Those on the far left will say that to do so is a social good. I have heard this sort of conceptual inanity repeatedly, and I have often asked for clarification. When asked what is meant by social good, left-wingers often mean "the public interest." When asked to define the public interest, they fumble, mumble, and twist themselves like linguistic pretzels into all orders of moral conundrums.

Society is nothing more than the sum of each individual person. Therefore, any reference to the public good would have to first logically refer to what is the good of each individual person. The answer to this presupposes the question—how do we know what that good is?

One of the glorious achievements of this country, and one that has appealed to millions the world over, is that we get to choose a conception of the good for ourselves. For some, it is having a family, and for others, it is pursuing a career or devoting one's life to a specialized hobby, service, or traveling—you name it. There are as many conceptions of the good as there are persons to imagine them. In America, the state has no business imposing any conception of the good on you or deciding *a priori* what your conception of the good ought to be. It leaves you free to choose your own notion of the good, so long as in doing so, you do not violate the inviolate rights of others. Any foisted notion of the public good on individuals means that a group of people has decided that their interests and their conception of the good should be the sum of the good of all members of society. It is an act of tyranny because it overrides your conscience and takes away your indubitable capacity to decide *what* the good is for you personally.

The cardinal sin of asking for anything for free is that you abnegate your responsibility not just for maintaining your existence but, more importantly, of achieving your humanity. For we achieve our humanity in several ways. One is by exchanging goods and services with others. We affirm the worth of the other, and we respect the other by rewarding him or her for such services, and, in so doing, our agency is implicated in affirming our self-worth and dignity in the beautiful act of reciprocity. In reciprocity, there is a recognition of equality among each of us as individuals; each ratifies the survival of the other through this reciprocation.

The moral question that must be posed to the welfare reparations recipient is this—what does it do to your moral life as a black person to be the permanent beneficiary of this form of altruism? It sends a paralyzing message to blacks that it is fundamentally misfortune, *simpliciter*, that gives them a right to rewards. The message that is transmitted is that it is not your efforts and initiative exercised on behalf of your life that are responsible for its upkeep; rather, it is your misfortune. And, as I have mentioned, this misfortune should be a mortgage on the purse strings of others. Any entitlement demand that stems from a sense of the unearned is basically an act of stealing value from another person. Since values are the products of the mind and of one's effort, and wealth is the material application of human values on earth, to accept the appropriated products of another person's mind is to engage in the nationalization and colonization of the mind of another person. It is *cognitive extortion*.

If people see misfortune, bad luck, or even cosmic injustice (theirs or anyone else's) as the fundamental justification for demanding reward, then they will inevitably come to disregard their creative capabilities—which have great emancipatory and restorative powers—as non-constitutive features of their identities. They will, inexorably, have been alienated from a fundamental sense of what it means to be a human being.

What I have described happening to blacks under the auspices of the Great Society programs of Lyndon Johnson and its welfare reparations satellite is what I believe is the beginning of a malaise in much of the black community—a cultural depression and lack of vitality. This vitality, this exuberance for and pride in struggle, was an omnipresent feature of the identity of many blacks prior to the passage of the 1964 Civil Rights Act.

Blacks had been placed in the historical process once they had been emancipated from slavery. From that moment on, their creative agency, even under conditions of oppression, had shone stunningly. Their capabilities had sprung forth, and they made significant cultural contributions to the republic of which they were a part, even if that republic had not entirely accepted them as full-fledged members of the American family. They were, for the most part, patriots; they strove to make something of their lives. They bore a consciousness of freedom in the form of radical self-actualization and evolution. By matriculating through the various iterations of the republic, they had acquired a form of self-consciousness that universalized their moral, political, and spiritual sensibilities.

E. B. Du Bois had placed great emphasis on blacks and whites sharing a proximal space in their grounding in Western history and culture. In *The Souls of Black Folk*, he declared that the heritage of the West was the heritage of all. He did not decry the wonders of Western civilization, and its creators did not decry or reject him either. He writes:

> "I sit with Shakespeare, and he winces not. Across the color line I move my arm with Balzac and Dumas, where smiling men and welcoming women glide in gilded halls. From out the caves of evening that swing between the strong-limbed earth and the tracery of the stars, I summon Aristotle and Aurelius and what soul I will, and they come all graciously with no scorn or condescension. So, wed with Truth, I dwell above the veil. Is this the life you grudge us, O knightly America? Is this the life you long to change into the dull red hideousness of Georgia? Are you so afraid lest peering from this high Pisgah between Philistine and Amalekite, we sight the Promised Land?"

This was the dream Du Bois had for blacks in America—a thoroughly integrated one. He envisioned a republic in which the political and moral sensibilities of blacks and whites, having been forged in the precepts and universal principles of Western civilization and the emancipatory tropes of the Enlightenment, would be marked for integration and success. Many blacks achieved just that, qualified not by the formal credentials from American institutions which, for the most part, kept them out, but by their resilience, grit, honor, tenacity, and the agency that comes from matriculating under the aegis of Western civilization and their tense relationship with the institutions of the republic in which they were slowly realizing and achieving their freedom.

The 1960s economic welfare programs were supplemented by a series of formal affirmative action programs that were themselves forms of reparations—these were attempts to include blacks in corporate and university institutions where they had been traditionally barred from entering. The verdict on whether those programs worked or not is still out on several fronts—many continue to argue that they helped white women and already qualified middle-class blacks more than they did poor and low-skilled blacks. Writers such as Shelby Steele and Thomas Sowell have addressed this point at great length, and readers are encouraged to explore their extant works on these topics.

Universities opened their doors to black students at unprecedented levels. It was now illegal for corporations to racially discriminate against blacks in hiring. Blacks constituted a protected class of citizens. These are reparative gestures white America has made since the 1960s towards black inclusiveness into mainstream society.

The wrong was righted. If there was a debt, it was being paid off.

But something was happening in large swaths in the black community. Officially and legally, the age of oppression was over. Blacks were living in an age of post-oppression. There were no legal barriers prohibiting them from pursuing their life goals. By 1972, it would be safe to say that the Age of White Supremacy was over. America no longer held an official ideology of the supremacy of the white race, and there were no laws explicitly preferring whites, or exclusionary or punitive of nonwhites simply on the grounds of race. Quite the opposite—the country was manufacturing a world in which blacks would become sacred icons and would be offered preferential treatment. It was an era where people were deliberately seeing race but in a new way—one in which they could recognize racism and combat it.

The official struggle for legal equality was over. All that was left was the challenge of assimilation and integration of blacks into the mainstream of American society.

However, this is where the beginning of the crisis in meaning and purpose in life began for several blacks. All their lives, their existence had been forged in painfully oppressive conditions, and yet few had claimed to be real victims, largely, one could argue, because such talk had no moral traction in a world that did not take the suffering of blacks seriously.

But that all changed with the civil rights movement and the passages of the Civil Rights Act. Martin Luther King Jr. had done something restorative and healing to a nation's conscience. He had played a significant role in not just embarrassing those who had not treated black suffering seriously, he had refrained from morally damning those who had mistreated blacks. He had equalized the two juxtaposing faces of humanity, reduced the moral, proximal distance between them, and equalized them. Their fractured humanity was made into a universal, moral, homogenous image—all human beings are deserving of equal treatment before the law, and all are to be respected for their inviolate moral worth.

King projected the image of a benevolent universe. He was a spiritual giant; he made friends out of foes. He neither sought revenge nor power and dominion over whites. He sought moral inclusion for all disenfranchised peoples and respect for the inalienability of their rights.

And that was still not enough for a lot of blacks, whose existential angst began to set in. A cult of existential death began to pervade black consciousness and would cushion a pathological ethos that would seek to denigrate Du Bois's dream. Self-segregation and turning one's back on the Enlightenment goal of universal inclusion would be replaced by a separatist, tribal logic that would seek to recast blacks as unknowable long-time sufferers and pure outsiders—all while being the recipients of reparative gestures and the beneficiaries of special programs.

Haunting, vexatious questions threatened the psychic lives of many blacks after the late civil rights era: "What do I do with my life when the 'cosmic deliverance quest,' which my existence had been searching for, has been finally delivered by the republic of the United States? What exactly am I supposed to do with my life now that the grand drama is over? How can I use my body and agency not just to raise a family and live a life in accordance with my value? How can I use my body as a weapon of something?"

In weaponizing the body, it would eventually become addicted to something that would ease the angst and the terrible rage and anger that erupted after freedom was achieved. Addiction to aid, as such, is one's only mode of survival. Logically, therefore, one always needs a financial bailout, the object of which becomes one's moral redeemer.

In this case, the moral redeemer is the all too embarrassed and guilty white liberal who feels a strange surge of power in his or her capacity to correct what is believed to be an almost cosmic injustice. Eager for redemption and atonement, this white emancipatory power shapes itself as a cosmic god. Its supremacy is addictive, seductive, and unchallenged. It is also very white.

Caught in a maelstrom of dependency, a desire for radical autonomy, and directionless sovereignty, rage that would manifest itself in street and campus riots and a degenerative form of self-segregation took hold of America in the latter part of the 1960s.

The university would be the place where blacks would wage a revolution. In the name of cultural reparations handed to them in the name of identity studies, they would unleash a lesser form of cognitive eugenics that threatens the very existence of our republic today. That revolution—in the form of cancel culture, social justice warriorship, woke culture, the war against free speech, and movements to abolish Western civilization in all spheres of education (our republic has morphed into cancel culture)—is cultural reparations handed to nihilistic revolutionaries intent on destroying America.

The most lethal and destructive of the revolutionaries would use their bodies as weapons of mass destruction on Western modes of knowing, of the canon, of reason, and everything that, heretofore, had constituted their moral and intellectual identity. Black Studies, as it was first called, would summon these metaphysical rebels and support a phalanx of weak, guilty, morally shame-filled, white, sycophantic university administrators. Obsequious Babbitts are what they were.

As we will come to see, these power-driven, semiliterate race hustlers, whose goal was power and wanton destruction of the knowledge based on which the United States, capitalism, and an individualism were defended, would eventually spawn a plethora of other activist disciplines. Their goal and ultimate victory were in the death and destruction of the American mind.

FOUR

Their Final Solution: The New Negritudes, Revolutionary Victim Studies, Black Nihilism, and the Abolition of "Whiteness"

S oon after tasting the victories of this moral eugenics program unleashed against whites' actual or imagined sins, blacks were voraciously hungry. They were also filled with anger and explosive rage. Gratitude was not an emotion they felt, as beneficiaries of the rights accorded them via the civil rights movements.

They were hungry for power—black power. They were hungry for revenge. They were hungry to assume the perpetual mantel of victims and the conferral of moral, iconic sainthood that came with it for the first time. The insignia of moral innocence that they would enjoy as a result of being seen as historical victims would give them a great deal of social capital—in fact, more social capital and political clout than they could have hoped for. Long after they had achieved that power, and after they had been emancipated from the bondage of legal disenfranchisement, too many of them squandered and wasted that capital. They are now on the verge of self-eviction from the realm of the historical process.

Many blacks are not only desirous of this power but are equally demanding that it be accompanied with an attendant guilt suffered by whites. It is the kind of guilt that is visited upon you when you realize that you have been told you're a rotten, mean-spirited bigot all your life. You're advised that you need to spend your life in search of repentance, acts of contrition, atonement, redemption, and ultimate salvation. In the end, short of annihilating your existence from this earth, there is nothing you can do about the black problem. The "abolition of whiteness" sloganeering that accompanies much of Critical Race Theory's normative agenda is, as I will show in detail, a euphemistic way of telling white people to terminate their lives.

Blacks smelled blood in turbulent waters of the late 1960s. They were navigating in a freer and more open society, and the blood they smelled was white guilt and embarrassment. There was no greater place to hand over the first installment of reparations—which I refer to as cultural reparations—to blacks than in our nation's universities. The new appropriators of cultural black power were not content to win a seat in universities from which they had been previously excluded. A cadre of race hustlers entered the academy, armed with a culturally and economically Marxist agenda to burn the system down and remake it in their own revolutionary style.

These blacks were not only filled with rage, they were consumed with resentment. Afrocentrism collided with the Black Power movements to reject traditional institutions that, in their views, had been agencies created under the auspices of imperial racist discourse. These Black Studies race hustlers, who would declare openly that they were fighting the false consciousness and enforced mind-colonization, wanted their own ways of validating their standpoint experiences. Theirs was a revolt against the principles of the Enlightenment and reason itself, which were taken to be constructs that were not only compatible with colonialism and "racist capitalism," but constitutive of them.

In *A Companion to African-American Studies*, Gordon and Gordon point out that the founding of Black Studies was influenced by the Black Panthers' goal of "decolonizing the minds of black people." They write: "African-American Studies is an intrinsically politicized unit of the academy whose objective is to overcome 'false consciousness' [a Marxist term, created by 'white supremacy']"—or, to put it differently, to understand what W. E. B. Du Bois called "the double consciousness," which, after the 1960s, was understood more as a contested truth.

We may say that the creation of the first "Victim Revolution Studies," or Black Studies, was revolutionary in that it was the first time that the American educational system deliberately instantiated and endorsed overt politicization of the classroom. It did so by setting up Black Nationalism in our nation's universities at the behest of whites who engaged in what was the first deliberate sign of not just undoing their racial stigma but of engaging in shameless acts of *virtue signaling*. This deferential act in turning the nation's classrooms into bastions of indoctrination centers and activist sites came at a cost, not just to educational pedagogy. Since social justice, canonical revisions, and propaganda were the foremost goals of the black programs in our universities, the traditional goals of academic rigor and cognitive development were sacrificed. Radical blacks almost embraced the principle of arrested intellectual development, since the standards of rigor, research, and qualitative judgments were viewed as couched in the white man's notions of ranking which pitted humans and groups against each other and led to "deplorable inequities."

The goal of Black Studies programs was not just to decolonize the minds of black students to reorient them away from a Europeanized model of thinking grounded in the value of the Enlightenment, universalism, and even a healthy dose of educational pluralism. These people, many of whom were mere semiliterate race hustlers, were strictly after power.

Black Studies, per se, was not a real discipline like philosophy, history, psychology, political science, English literature, or sociology. It had no methodology and, pedagogically speaking, it was intellectually bankrupt.

Let us be clear as to what we mean when we say that a discipline has a methodology to support it; it has a foundational anchor to give it coherence, sensibility in the literal sense, and the ability to yield conclusions and make judgments that are intelligible, comprehensible, and perceptible to the average human mind. When we talk about methodology, we mean a format or design that is an established process or the development of an objective procedure for carrying out research. The rules and procedures cannot be arbitrary and subjective; they must be consonant with the nature of each discipline. It is inappropriate for a literary scholar to use the methods employed by a physicist to analyze nineteenth century Victorian poetry. There are specific techniques used to identify, select, process and analyze information about a particular topic. Criteria for appraising validity and reliability are developed via a proper methodology.

But Black Studies was a Victims Revolution Studies agenda. The goal was activism and to establish Black Power.

In his anthropologically rich book, *The Victims' Revolution: The Rise of Identity Studies and the Closing of the Liberal Mind*, Bruce Bawer reconstructs much of what I have stated above. He observes that at San Francisco State University there was something called the Experimental College, where students were allowed to teach their own courses, which invariably turned informal rap sessions into formal courses. Heavily aligned with Black Panther and Marxist politics, the sweep of these programs over the country had the full backing of white college administrators, from university presidents to provosts and deans. In my view, these programs ought to be seen as a form of cultural reparations on the part of white American taxpayers.

The conservative writer Shelby Steele recalls his early days as a creator of the Black Studies program. He describes the people who started it as dummies—street guys who just came to hustle. There were people like Leonard Jeffries who, despite a long and pernicious anti-white and anti-Semitic philosophy, served as the Chairman of the Black Studies Department at City University of New York (CUNY). Steele describes him as an out-and-out hustler.

This has been the story of Black Studies—race hustlers and hucksters, semiliterate, street savvy race pimps who knew how to con white administrators out of hundreds of thousands of dollars for lucrative careers for themselves. In Bawer's *The Victims' Revolution*, Steele reports that it did not matter what these curricula consisted of because there were no oversight authorities seriously looking at what was taught. "Slipshod and jerry-built" is how Steele describes them. They eventually, of course, took over English departments. Today, it's all about ethnicity and racism. Later on, we'll look at just how the Black Studies programs of the sixties established the pernicious, anti-intellectual standard that permitted Rutgers University to declare, in 2020, that grammar is racist and that it would be focusing on critical grammar, that is, black English. In fall of the same year, the University of Chicago would go even further and refuse to allow any of its incoming doctoral students in English a place unless their studies incorporated some hodgepodge of social justice linked to black lives.

I'd like to continue my thesis that Black Studies programs were, and continue to be, a form of cultural reparations. This is premised on my larger argument that the 1964 Civil Rights Act has been participating in a series of incremental, reparative acts directed towards black American uplift.

Black Studies was a form of cultural reparations and not just because it was conducted under the auspices of administrative bodies run by powerful white people who funneled thousands of dollars into this fake discipline. It was because these bureaucratic bodies sanctioned the well-publicized agenda of these victims and their activist, revolutionary studies phenomena that would grant moral license for the creation of Women's Studies, Post-Colonial Studies, Queer Studies, Fat Studies, Disabilities Studies, Chicano Studies, and congeries of other programs, heavily indexed to post-modernism and cultural Marxism as their philosophical grid.

And what, exactly, was the revolutionary mission of Black Studies? It was not justice. King and the civil rights movement had fought to win blacks places at the top universities to integrate and assimilate them into the larger spheres of the American culture, so they could achieve economic parity with their compatriots. The race hustlers—and even genuine activists—were out for revenge. They wanted to get even by overthrowing the system. In the spirit of Frantz Fanon, they wanted to substitute one species of mankind with another. This endeavor inevitably sets out to change the order of the world. It is putatively an agenda for chaos.

The substitution of one species of mankind with another was framed by an agenda which set out to decolonize black people from white and Western educational paradigms. The semiliterate racial pimps and hustlers were academic activists inspired by the Black Panthers' ethos, which they sought to emulate and promulgate inside the classroom. This ethos translated into literal form was the creation of a new type of human being, who would be an atavistic, non-American black nationalist filled with racial pride, besotted with power and a maniacal will to impose his agenda on the rest of America. The Black Power ethos that charged Black Studies was fueled by a view that saw white Americans as colonists. America was an imperial, colonial empire with "outposts" within its borders. The colonized blacks had been in such a state since 1619, when the first slave ship arrived in Virginia, they claimed. In truth, that first ship contained not slaves but indentured servants.

The way in which these new Negritudes stood in diametric opposition to what King had advocated and fought for must be emphasized. Waiting in the wings for the imprimatur of official freedom—that is, no legal barriers to prevent them from pressing rights claims—they co-opted and bullied an obsequious set of cowardly, bureaucratic Babbitts into submitting to their demands all over the United States. Student strikes at a broad swath of universities such as Harvard, Yale, Cornell, Columbia,

Howard, and Amherst had a coercive effect and forced terrified administrators into establishing Black Studies programs. Between 1967–1968, eleven of the eighteen California colleges underwent some form of student activism, which ranged from uprooting trees and setting fires to outright physical violence. By 1969, most major American universities had Black Studies programs on their campuses.

These cultural reparations programs meant to assuage the anger, rage, and nihilistic impulses of students, who had just been the beneficiaries of a painful and protracted civil rights struggle, were generally not seen as educational programs but as an ideological indoctrination. It was the beginning of the national self-esteem movement. Self-esteem and self-respect would come from pride in race. The programs were not designed to foster better interracial relations or understanding; they were deeply regressive in nature, atavistic in their desire for racial separatism.

According to Maulana Ron Karenga, a founder of the discipline and author of *Introduction to Black Studies*, Black Studies was a badly needed and corrective of "traditional white studies," which he claimed would always be "inadequate and injurious in its omission and/or distortion of the lives and culture of the majority of humankind, especially the fathers and mothers of humankind and human civilization, African people."

According to Bawer, historically black colleges had always taught a rigorous curriculum of "Negro History." However, readers need to understand the purveyors of Black Studies were not interested in intercollegiate dialogue. In the minds of its advocates, it was a bunker shelter—a place for them to propagate myths about a lost, stupendous African civilization and hide behind a mirage of self-protective rhetoric, anger, and activism directed at the system while creating an alternative universe inside in which to hide.

I think it was the beginning of the coddling of the American mind by progressive white power brokers and administrators who felt guilty for the injustice blacks had suffered by members of their race.

INVERTED LIBERAL WHITE SUPREMACY

I think also it was an inverted form of white supremacy on the part of these seemingly obsequious white liberals. If they could create an underclass of undereducated blacks, who would really never achieve parity in the outside world with their white compatriots, then they would retain their managerial plantation lordship over those that would always constitute an underclass.

These advocacy and non-intellectual activist programs would be a way for black students to hunker down into a sheltered sense of security. They constituted an alternative reality in which their diatribes and rants could bewitch, terrify, and effect a new reality because they could simply will it. It was an escapist universe where they would not have to deal with white people on any terms but their own; it was also an escape into their own hermetically sealed, ideological silos that could not be challenged. In several programs, whites were actively discouraged from enrolling in such courses.

In many respects, after the arduous and fair-minded appeal to the goodness in whites to do the right thing and treat blacks with the same dignity and sense of moral worth as they would themselves that King had implored his fellow citizens to abide by, the violence, exploitation, and coercion that accompanied the balkanizing of our universities by Black Studies programs was a massive con pulled on much of white America and those blacks who didn't dream of resegregation and separatism. They simply wanted to participate as equals with their compatriots in the new world that the Civil Rights Act had opened up for them. Those blacks were being conned out of a future in their own way and because they possessed a desire to challenge themselves intellectually and apply the highest scholastic standards of excellence to their work and lives, they were being drawn into an educational ghetto.

For the most part, the runners of Black Studies programs demanded to be autonomous, fiscally well-endowed, and with full departmental status. It was important that they bypass traditional understandings of what was recognized as legitimate academic work by making a connection with and having a large impact on the black community in a significant way. They also were granted rights to award PhDs.

Whites were granting cultural and, through employment, economic reparations to a phalanx of activist scholars who were introducing the notion of standpoint epistemology via postmodernism. This was the view that ways of knowing and perceiving the world are determined solely by one's lived experience and identity, say, as a black person, gay man or woman, or Native American. Further, cognitive access to one's way of knowing by outsiders was virtually impossible. There could be no objective way of appraising the viewpoints of those outside your kin group. This reasoning relied on a specious notion of ethical relativism— the idea that there are no objective and universal criteria for adjudicating among disputing truth claims. If moral relativism advances this idea then its ruling principle is *subjectivism*—what one *feels* is the truth constitutes the truth. Logic and reason, according to the more radical school of subjectivism, is the creation of racist and imperialist white constructs. But if nihilism is the logical concomitant of relativism, one must now ask: what is the philosophical foundation of relativism? What first foundational principles underscore the relativism that gives rise to the nihilism in educational systems that promote standpoint epistemology?

That school of thought is *postmodernism*. If you want to see the connection between calls for a decolonized syllabus and indiscriminate vandalism of all statues because they are simply representations of the past and of men of a racial orientation, and if you want to see metaphysical rage directed at everyone but no one in particular, look no further than the school of postmodernism—a vicious anti-reason and, therefore, anti-life phenomenon that robs human beings of a particular method of cognition. It deprives them of integrating fundamental principles to clear and lucid thinking that leads to intelligible and reasonable actions. It cuts away at the idea of an objective reality and replaces it with an unbridled and amorphous, necrotic lump of feelings that are treated as tools of cognition. However, these feelings are only the fears, prejudices, and projections of chronically anxious people for whom truth is a death knell, as it emancipates them from their self-curated silos and forces them into a universe that cares only about facts, not feelings or wishful thinking.

Hence, today, hacking mindlessly at statues, "decolonizing courses," and ridding educational courses of canonical, dead white educators cannot magically bring about a new world order, and the perpetrators know it. So, they resort to wanton destruction and nihilism. Ideas have consequences; further, all actions, even nihilistic ones, are antecedently traceable back to some philosophical set of principles. Postmodern nihilism is the ruling school of thought guiding human actions today and destroying our civilization. Its ruling principles deserve to be elucidated and delineated clearly.

We may begin by contrasting it with the philosophy of the Enlightenment. This was a movement that sought to understand the world and humanity on a rational basis. Its fundamental premise states that human experience, whether in the natural world or in social life, is accessible to human reason and explicable in rational terms. It is equally accessible to all persons, regardless of their existential differences. The Enlightenment project promulgated the idea that reason can locate truth with calendrical exactitude that is accessible to all human beings, regardless of tribal, ascriptive identity. Its humanistic, philosophic systems provided the legal, moral, and political vocabularies for the abolition of slavery and the inclusion of persons who had been excluded from the community within the domain of the ethical, and it admits another truism—moral learning does occur. It motivates the ethical behaviors of those who are driven to end oppression and injustice wherever they find them.

Postmodernism, on the other hand, is a disciplinary movement that questions the validity of modern science and offers strong resistance to any truth claims. Its defenders assert that truth claims are discriminatory and oppressive on the grounds that they are totalizing, hegemonic, and definitive. However, truth claims proven to be true are just those things; they become universal and prescriptive for all human beings, based on our shared, rational nature.

Postmodernism rejects humanism and, above all, rejects what I would term as the greatest moral, political achievement in history—representative liberal democracy. It hails a decentering approach to all spheres of life or knowledge.

Decentering refers to an absence of everything at the center of a thought system or any overriding truth. It prefers concentrating at the margins. It privileges a form of skepticism that has little to do with suspending judgment until further evidence or judicious analysis and inspection of evidence reveal truth. It adopts an antifoundational stance that discounts profound, qualitative differences among viewpoints and then champions equal treatment.

This, of course, exists in theory only. With a hysterical virulence, unusual in those who champion skepticism and tolerance, emotion-driven factionalism is the logical outcome of postmodernism's anticonceptual approach to issues. Its defenders will assert that any offense to their sensibilities is evil and must be expunged from the universe. Viewpoints and their attendant materialization as actions in the world are justified by an appeal to private feelings and personal experiences. Postmodernism disqualifies objective appraisers from judging any viewpoint and actions in the world ethically. The postmodernist recommendation of a multitude of incompatible juxtaposed logics, all in perpetual movement without the possibility of permanent resolution, results in chaos. It fosters a culture in which whims, caprices, fiats, and feelings serve as the only fundamental criteria for legitimizing "truth" and actions. External appraisal is seen as a form of macroaggression when applied to actions committed by groups and microaggression when formulated against individuals.

With a multiplicity of divergent logics, incommensurable and irreconcilable systems, we can see that postmodernism provides a convenient cover for any subjective and personal quest for power, violation of rights, and basic human lawlessness. Even the concept of law is regarded as an oppressive construct designed by those who wish to exercise dominion over the marginalized.

When an individual or group's behavior or philosophic viewpoint is evaluated by objective criteria governed under the invariable laws of logic, persons rendering judgments are indicted on charges of cognitive imperialism and sometimes racism. Too often, they are deemed culturally disqualified to make moral judgments against those who fall outside their racial, ethnic, or national group.

By default and by design, the end result of this philosophy is nihilism and political or psychological anarchy. Today, in the form of not just these but in manifestations of cancel culture, endless accusations of cultural appropriation, and successful efforts to suppress offending speech, we are witnessing the wholesale death of our civilization. The result, if not challenged, is beyond nihilism, myopic parochialism, and shrunken imaginations. Because this philosophy is an attack against individualism, reason, progress, and the notion of truth itself, its deadliest consequence is a form of moral inversion of human beings.

The process by which we become moral inverts is made possible by two factors. The first is by consciously resorting to a presocialized entity that evacuates the moral attributes that suffuse the soul and without which we become feral animals. The second is more common, and it occurs by default or by conscious intent. It is to ingest the philosophic principles of a belief system that constitutes an erosion of moral identity. Postmodernism, by casting aspersion and crippling skepticism on values as such, is a death philosophy.

In the West, it is important not just to rediscover the Enlightenment values that have informed our republic and crafted moral personalities in all of us. We must consciously find those who are purveyors of this deadly moral virus and extinguish them in ways that are legal but culturally and morally forceful.

We must stop being apologists for Enlightenment values, inoculate ourselves with them, and, with implacable certainty, advance and enforce those values that enable us to flourish and thrive. We will be surprised at how soon our adversaries will be felled, largely because their survival relied on our silence and willful sanction of their ethically bankrupt systems. Few today fight for the virtues of individualism, respect for the inviolable and inalienable rights of people to be sovereign and self-governing entities, and the unassailable, universal first principles that apply to all human beings. It is the philosophy that founded the United States and the unquestionable commitment to respecting the intrinsic dignity and moral worth of each person who gets said worth and value from God that must be adhered to categorically.

Armed with both a Marxist sensibility and the nihilistic ethos of postmodernism, the practitioners of Black Studies knew that cultural reparations would be best accomplished not by national recognition of achievements made by blacks or having a national museum that would detail the real and historic achievements made by blacks in fields of science, medicine, technology, literature, and art. The power of individual black people is not *racial* achievements—they are the achievements of people who just happen to be black. In fact, the celebratory scenario I described of black individuals would not be a form of reparations or of collective black power. It would be inextricably interwoven into the fabric of American culture, where the achievements themselves would be symbolic encomiums of American greatness and patriotism, inseparable from American folklore and a non-revisionist historical record.

The promulgators of postmodernism, moral relativism, and, as we shall see, purveyors of a formal Afro-pessimistic nihilism movement knew that universities are the transmission belt of a culture's ideas and ideals via the intellectual vanguards who rule its turf.

They were not interested in the old, bourgeois practice of celebrating objective "Negro History," as was to be found in historically black universities and colleges. Under the stewardship of white accomplices who thought they were righting a wrong by handing autonomy to a broad swath of blacks who claimed they and only they had the right to be in charge of the narratives that depicted them, they related their history and framed their own experiences.

Such blacks were treading dangerous waters; they were re-enacting the drama of their ancestral indigenes. Only this time, they were pitting themselves against a newly imagined white phantom they thought was there to steal their past and distort their history. They had no history to steal, only agency to be expropriated by liberal, white supremacists, who beguiled others into seeing them as a guilt-ridden, masochistic group of contrite penitents in search of redemption.

This phenomenon was occurring at the moment in history when white guilt, operating at such a degree, would have left the guilty bureaucrats in charge of the histories of any marginalized peoples bereft of capacity to micromanage such histories—they would simply wait patiently for the spiritual casualties at the end of this educational farce to start emerging. Deliberately making caricatures of themselves and distorting all traditional framing prisms and methodological procedures pertaining to research and scholarship, the new Negritudes were taking themselves outside the historical process by resurrecting a new kind of racial primitivism predicated on wishful thinking and racial fantasies of a lost paradisial past. The sub-Saharan regions from which they were descendant had no historical glories, no literary, technological, scientific, or political equivalent of Medieval Europe or even Europe during its darkest ages.

White America helped to pay the debt they thought was owed to black America by participating in the epistemological and historical sham on which Black Studies was predicated. However, if white America had subjected blacks to a Manichean binary identity, where blackness stood for inferiority and, *a fortiori*, ground for exclusion from the mainstream republic from which they could see no reprieve, the new Negritudes were reversing that trend and applying it unilaterally across American universities to remake a new humanity—a revolutionary, pro-masculinist, almost feral will-to-power, legitimized and executed by racial association. It was pure witch doctory, similar to that of the primitive and atavistic thuggery and expression of white supremacy and its satellite ideological architects such as the Ku Klux Klan.

I submit that, in the wake of the civil rights movement and its aftermath and at a point in history when Martin Luther King Jr.'s universal message of love and integration and a cosmopolitan spirit of fraternity and nonracial solidarity (solidarity in causes of universal injustice) was a viable option for ethical life and living, black nationalists, with the help of progressive white Americans, were instantiating a deep and divisive form of cultural nationalism that lingers on today.

Moral Identity Theft

The new Negritudes were not integrationists or assimilationists. They were separatists—culturally and existentially. The philosophical means by which they put this agenda to work was by way of moral appropriation, and by adhering to it, they became promulgators of racial momism and polylogism.

Simply put, a moral appropriator is a person who tries to extract moral value by illicit means. In much the same way that a social climber creates the impression of possessing class, status, and pedigree by displaying markers that are interpreted by society as signifying these coveted impressions, so the moral appropriator tries to gain standing, not by achieving a moral status earned through a character cultivated by moral actions, but by riding on the prestige of a title with which he self-identifies.

A social climber may associate with wealthy individuals, including celebrities and those with fancy social titles, in the hope that, through such associations, others will come to see him as having the coveted features of his friends. Ultimately, he hopes they'll bestow the status he so desperately craves. Through his association with these friends, he is allowed to bypass the long road they may—or may not—have taken in order to achieve their status. This is because the social climber does not believe that he has the requisite capabilities to pursue his goals and, more importantly, because he (for whatever reason) would rather take shortcuts and create a deceptive facsimile to communicate as authentic, which others take to be genuine.

The moral appropriator also comes in several guises, from the great pretender to the serial confessor who believes that a combination of confessions and good deeds will win him righteous pride of place in the registers of society's prized conventions.

Through his behavior and attitude towards his kin group and those outside of it, the racial tribalist is a moral appropriator *writ large.* There are two examples that best amplify this phenomenon. One is the obsession some individuals have in extolling their own worth not by means of their individual achievements but by harking back to a "Great Past" mythology. What the individuals cannot attain through their personal achievements, they acquire by virtue of their membership in an imagined, mythic culture whose distinctness lies in its great past. This is communicated by a mythical narrative that portrays it as the great contributor to human civilization in a way unequalled by other civilizations. Often, it originated as a creation myth; hence, all other civilizations or cultures are mere derivatives of this original First People and culture. Manufacturers of the great myth interpret and reinterpret the present to ensure that it accords with a reality that, although lacking remnants visibly present in contemporary culture, still retains its most fundamental features, thus ensuring each member a share in that greatness and an exalted share in humanity and personal worth that comes from membership in the group linked with the great past.

The second example in which the tribalist functions as a moral appropriator is in being what we may call an *ethnic revivalist* or *ethnic romantic*. These are individuals who are many generations removed from their ancestral roots but who desperately seek some affiliation with those roots.

The case of black Americans is a special one deserving of separate commentary. For the most part, those labeled as black or African American have not voluntarily identified themselves as such. The racial taxonomy used to pick out such individuals has a long and interesting history. The terms used historically have included but have not been restricted to *coloreds, colored people, colored Americans, Negrosaxons, AfraAmericans, race men, non-whites, negroes, Negroes, blacks, Afro-Americans* and *black Americans.* Individuals with such identifiers are not as autonomous in holding them as are those bearing the labels German American or Irish American—the latter being voluntary signifiers that individuals in these respective groups are free to adopt or drop at any moment. In other words, whether those terms are used to mark out any specific individual is largely a matter of choice. This is not the case for African Americans, many of whom prefer the terms black or people of color but are denied public usage of such terms. As the author of one classic study in sociology argued: "If one believes one is part English and part German and identifies in a survey as German, one is not in danger of being accused of trying to 'pass' as non-English and of being 'redefined' English by the interviewer. But if one were part African and part German, one's self-identification as German would be highly suspected and probably not accepted if one 'looked' black according to the prevailing social norms."

My goal is to show how those aspiring to tribal terms, when they are generationally removed from them because their participation in the history and traditions of the "people" is minimal, are committing a category mistake. What makes you African if you don't speak the language of those spoken on the continent, have never visited African countries, were not born there, and lack a sustained relationship to the cultural phenomena associated with being African?

It also shores up, on close examination, the questionable motives such individuals have for labeling themselves as they do. It is more than just a category mistake that people are making—they are attempting to ride on the social prestige of an identity that bears little resemblance to who they are in their day-to-day lives.

This is why I have argued that the tribalist is not capable of portraying people as they are but only as caricatures—all are reduced to a formulaic set of attributes that is established early on in his perception of an individual. This allows the tribalist the capacity to prejudge individuals. He can do this because they are a confirmation of what he knew before he meets them. They are good, solid, productive, clean, and upright persons if they are from his group; they are untrustworthy, dangerous, sly, and contaminable if they are from another. The scale of negativity of his judgment depends on the degree of scorn he has for the particular group from which the person he is judging is a member.

The tribalist is not interested in whether his judgments are true or false or whether his appraisal of a person's character corresponds to reality, i.e., whether these are the behaviors and traits that manifest themselves in this person's life. If they fail to manifest such traits, the tribalist will not tell himself that she is an anomaly or an aberration; he'll say that these authentic traits are simply lying dormant, and the individual is guilty of mimicry. He or she is acting white, or assuming Germanic characteristics that are the opposite of vulgar, crude, Slavic impulses he harbors if he is Serbian, or trying to be a gentleman, if he is Croatian and the tribalist is Serbian. To the tribalist, the manifestation of traits that do not correspond to his preconceived portrait are viewed suspiciously. The person in question is masking who she really is; her true self lies dormant beneath the thin veneer of false characteristics being exhibited, and only the omniscient and infallible tribalist, acting like a wholesaler as opposed to a retailer in the realm of character analysis, can know that self.

Why waste time getting to know the personality of each individual who belongs to a group? A national, racial, or ethnic character-type forms the essence of every individual. To waste time looking for individuality is to seek out the accidental and the incidental as far as the tribalist is concerned. Sooner or later, the person will display the traits that mark his tribal character-type—sooner or later every Roma will steal from you, every Jew will "Jew you out of your penny, like the conniving entrepreneurs that they are," "every Arab will erupt in implacable rage at some provocation," and "every Italian American is somehow connected to the mob."

In essence, the strong tribalist is a *racial subjectivist*. Racial subjectivism is the view that an individual's racial constitution determines "his mental processes, his intellectual outlook, his thought patterns, his feelings, his conclusions—and that these conclusions, however well established, are valid only for members of a given race, who share the same underlying constitution." According to one Nazi, knowledge and truth are peculiarities that originate in specific forms of consciousness and are attuned exclusively to the specific essence of their mother consciousness. Each race, therefore, creates its own truth and exists in its own universe.

In his book, *The Ominous Parallels: The End of Freedom in America*, Leonard Peikoff notes that human beings of different races are separated by an unbridgeable, epistemological gulf, according to this subjectivist logic. This makes it impossible for them to communicate or resolve disputes peacefully.

Carl Schmitt, a leading Nazi theorist, noted that: "An alien may be as critical as he wants to be…he may be intelligent in his endeavor, he may read books and write them, but he thinks and understands things differently because he belongs to a *different kind*, and he remains within the existential conditions of his own kind in every decisive thought."

The new black nationalist and their intellectual analog in the universities embraced a principle we may refer to as polylogism, which is the ruling principle of the racial subjectivist. That is, the idea that each group—Aryan, British, and Jew—has its own truth, logic, and distinct method of reasoning. Each group has a unique mental structure that is valid for its own group and invalid for other groups. What is most noteworthy is that thinkers from the same race will ask similar questions and seek answers and solutions in the exact same direction.

This sense of belonging to a different kind is the intractable belief that is tenaciously held by strong tribalists. Psychologically, to belong to a different kind is to be existentially ensconced in a world with ready-made meaning, values, and purpose. One can invest this world with an assemblage of who one is, but that assemblage is already drawn from the ethnoracial/national caste of which one is a part.

The strong tribalist is spared the burden of having to be original. He is original, but his originality comes from the *sui generis* nature of his tribe—his particular kind. Because there is no other tribe like his tribe, membership is a constitutive feature of his identity, and *he* is a constitutive member of the tribe, the existential burden of cosmic insignificance that is the lot of many persons is one that he is spared. He lives in a cosmos without which life would be unimaginable, and also one in which, without him, there would be a loss, since he comes to see himself as a valuable part that makes up the type that is his particular kind. To belong to multiple "different kinds" is to exist in an existential wasteland; it is to be everywhere and nowhere in particular. One is not only lost—there is no real home to find, since one's mind and body are allocated and dispersed among different *kinds.*

The problem, however, before Black Studies aspired to a universalist agenda through its multiple cross-listings with other departments, was that it remained insular and self-perpetuating as the exclusive domain of victimized blacks. Whites, no matter how progressive they were or aspired to be, were not invited to participate in this new enterprising field forged in the manacles of victimization with a moral twist. Standing on its own petard,

Black Studies—like women's Studies, Chicano Studies, Queer Studies, Post-Colonial Studies, and later on, Fat Studies and White Studies—was deeply anchored in a psychological matrix. The goal of the program was not just to assert the humanity of people whose humanity had been denigrated. It was to make its people feel good about themselves. The goal was not just consciousness awareness, but self-esteem by association with ancestral members of one's race (or kind) whose achievements were meant to diffuse, in the minds of the white majority, the idea that people of color were underachievers and incapable of intellectual substance. This is understandable psychologically, but as a disciplinary objective, it had serious consequences. Because the impetus for its creation was reactionary—to fight what it still believed was white supremacy, both culturally and scholastically. The discipline, like most multicultural studies, occupied too narrow a conceptual space to properly qualify as an academic field. Several of the topics were (and remain) frivolous, with discussions ranging from black hair to the politics of rap music. Anything and everything pertaining to black life was grist for academic inquiry. This, too, was the case for queer studies and other multicultural studies, departments, or programs.

The truth of the matter with such studies was the narcissism that defined them. It was blacks' raciated bodies and souls that were at the center of inquiry, rather than the dispassionate study of a field of inquiry. A metaphysics of black embodiment became the arbiter of "competing epistemologies." To be black (and to be woman, Chicano/Latino/Native American, and lesbian/gay, among others) was to know in a specific way that was antipodal to other ways of knowing.

Victims Revolution Studies, therefore, didn't pejoratively compete with each other, since all recognized that a subjective logic amenable to them and them only was the proper mode of cognition. Since their epistemologies as embodied subjects were different, there were competing epistemologies among the multicultural studies units. We refer to them in this way since they presented competing truth claims on account of human reality. These truth claims do not have shared evaluative standards, but, facing innumerable, epistemological quandaries, they simply posit a humanity that is unique to each member of different subgroups.

Chicano embodiment and black embodiment were two different realms of subjective social reality, whose concomitant, differing epistemologies needn't clash violently because they were not competing for the same universal human agency. Black, gay, and Chicano agency were different as opposed to, say, the generic "human agency," purported by the architects of the Western Enlightenment project and its objectivist canon. These victimologists could hear each other's stories and exchanges of what it was like to be an embodied agent of a specific species type, but since each was not trying to remake the other into the image of the other's type, they need not become enemies. It was the traditional, universal canon, or rather its purveyors and practitioners, that were the enemies. Those who tried to abstract from human differences and radical experiences using a single strand known as reason, while simultaneously showing that some members from different groups lacked in it, were those who had been dehumanized and excluded from the human domain. They were the subjects of the multicultural studies victim programs who would form a new human community.

Since they had not made the initial cut in the "cult of humanity," they had to manufacture their own humanities and sense of agency based on a belief in the subjectivism of reality. They proclaimed that objective reality is that which had stifled them, since they could never aspire to be part of the laws of nature that defined it and those who fell under its conceptual rubric. Reality, therefore, had to be malleable, subjective, non-absolute, fluid, and plastic. It had to become an indeterminate realm that could be contested and changed by the consciousness of those perceiving it.

The ruling principle in all Victim Revolution Studies departments was racial, ethnic, and sexual subjectivism. This is worth repeating for emphasis. In one form or another, such subjectivists believe that an individual's inborn racial, ethnic, and sexual constitution determines his or her mental processes, intellectual outlook, thought patterns, feelings, and conclusions. Such conclusions are valid only for the members of the race, ethnos, and sexually determined—however well established—and valid only for a member of a given species type who shares the same underlying racial, national, or ethnic constitution. Knowledge and truth are peculiarities that originate in particular forms of consciousness and are attuned to the specific essence of their mother consciousness. Each race, ethnic group, and sexual species creates its own truth and universe. They are separated by an unbridgeable, epistemological gulf according to this subjectivist logic. As a result, communication or resolution of disputes becomes difficult or even impossible.

It is on the grounds of this impossibility of a separatist tribal logic that the Black Studies departments, aided by other systemic, nihilistic models of activist scholarship, sought to undermine the liberal, educative mission of the nation's universities.

And what did cultural reparations look like? It was in effect a precursor to today's cancel culture, with black students reintroducing segregationist demands in their programs that not only excluded whites from participating but introduced often random, arbitrary, and non-vetted disparate congeries of black artists, writers, and manufactured philosophers into black-only domains of inquiry—just so long as they passed a litmus test of racial authenticity.

The times have changed only slightly. We have blacks who have instituted an annual day of absence at Evergreen State College, in which minority students and faculty previously met off campus to discuss campus issues and how to make the college more supportive of students. That later changed when the black racist students proclaimed that, on the day of absence, they wanted white people to stay off campus. When a white biology professor refused to comply and complained that people should "put phenotype" aside, he was threatened with his life and calls were made by student activists for his dismissal.

A new self-imposed segregation has struck like a funky epidemic across campuses. In yet another gesture of shameful appeasement to racist demands by black students for yet more racial self-segregation, New York University recently opened negotiations with students to create black resident floors on campus beginning in 2021. A "themed engagement floor" for black students is being advanced by a group called "Black Violets NYU." The group has complained that the overwhelming presence of white students has made it difficult for black students "to connect." Black Violets has also called for more black professors in its politics department and for the creation of a black student lounge on campus.

In June 2020, students at Rice University demanded that it fund a "non-residential Black House" on campus. They also wanted a statue of the university's founder removed. Other demands included that new students' requests for black roommates be met during orientation weeks; this demand is clearly at odds with federal civil rights laws. Other demands included that course descriptions have tags indicating what race and ethnic groups are involved, since several titles did not make it clear if diverse perspectives were offered in their course materials.

In June 2017, Harvard University held separate commencement ceremonies for black graduate students. One hundred and twenty students attended the third LatinX commencement ceremony replete with Latin music. Emory University and Henry College held diversity and inclusion year-end ceremonies. The University of Delaware joined a growing list with "Lavender" graduations.

By the time this book is published, there will be a multiplicity of schools meeting mostly new black students' demands for special black student lounges, all-black dorms, black seating spaces in cafeterias, and more spaces such as we witnessed at Evergreen University—where white people are expelled from campuses for several days so that black students can have a time on campus to feel special as "black people." What next? All black libraries with only black authors, black gyms, and black professors teaching only black students to avoid the racial trauma of being taught by a white instructor? If you think this is hyperbolic, observe that one of the demands made by black students at Rice University is that the school hire more black counselors and therapists and that they be trained in how to handle racial trauma.

I believe some thoughtful analysis is required here, especially as I have been a professor for almost twenty-five years. I have taught at two Ivy League universities, and I have taught poor kids from the cornfields of Indiana and Illinois and poverty-stricken black kids from East St. Louis.

No student at any elite university in this country, whether he or she be black, queer, immigrant, or transgendered, is marginalized. Also, can anyone imagine what life will be like for a black student with a degree from an elite university like NYU? One simple word—fabulous. He or she will probably never have to apply for a job and will be recruited midway through her senior year, long before any white student has even completed his or her final exam.

Such students are pampered with high-end scholarships, treated like royalty with their every need catered to, and every perceived slight they might feel is anticipated and solved long before it might have arisen in their consciousness.

Progressive American universities are the least racist to these radical left-wing students. Their peers and the various administrative bodies who run the universities are likely to prostrate themselves like obsequious Babbitts before them—and not just in meeting their tyrannical demands for exceptional treatment, but in feeling inordinate guilt that such students report feeling uneasy about their place in the universities.

So, what is this demand for racial segregation all about? To begin with, it is a disgraceful exercise in racist, reactionary politics and an egregious display of misanthropic behavior. At the heart of it is not just the practice of the Big Lie—that they are victims—but a preternatural conmanship at work. These students are racial hucksters exploiting white guilt and moral embarrassment for power and money. There are white university administrators who need to engage in some twisted, masochistic play with the sadistic whippings of privileged, entitled, black narcissistic students who, having been granted an enormous deal of institutional power, *know*, not feel, that the world does really revolve around them and will capitulate to their demands. It makes no difference if the world refuses because they, as anointed victims, who have the permanent *imprimatur* of innocence by default, are certified moral icons who exist beyond the reaches of criticism.

They have been encouraged by the institution to not just feel welcomed on campus, but to treat the university as an extension of their living rooms and the homes from which they come. There were no white people in those rooms and homes, so why should they now have to live in the real world and engage and live among white people?

Their tribal, separatist logic and the attendant trauma they report feeling is a charade. These students act like biological collectivists; that is, as if their whole mode of being in the world, their values, principles, terms of engagement, is governed by some internal form of chemical predestination. But it is not.

What they face is a post-oppressive age, one that treats them as full-fledged human beings—and they can't stand it. A deep existential crisis and a chronic sense of anxiety afflict them in such a world because…well, it is drama-free. It's just ordinary. Though they are feted and treated like royalty on these elite campuses, what they truly want is a universe in which they can command power and, inversely, create racist institutions.

Yes, on today's elite college campuses, discrimination exists towards conservative thinkers and their ideas. God help you if you're a patriotic American who is pro-capitalism and pro-individual rights, a First Amendment and Second Amendment absolutist, a critic of the welfare state, a lover of Israel, and a critic of Islamic Jihadists. But that hardly describes the Marxist-inspired, Black Lives Matter-motivated black separatists and racial, self-segregationist reactionaries.

Today, these students, their administrative appeasers, and the professors who have schooled them in their schemata, are the *purveyors* of institutional racism—not its victims. They have consciously weaponized their blackness and white guilt as a means of silencing criticism. They wish to harken back to some atavistic period when the black body was viewed as some amorphous, homogenized shaping of a majestic Nubian culture that, today, in our institutions of higher learning, will revolutionize thought, from decolonizing courses and ridding them of all European white thinkers, to declaring grammar, logic, and now even math, as racist to abolishing history departments because history itself is believed to be a fabrication of mythologies and not a codification of objective facts. The very faculty that distinguishes us from every other creature and makes man a human being—*reason*—is being called into question as a social construct meant to erase the identities of marginalized people.

This weaponized black body foists itself upon the world as a moral axiom from which all subsequent truth claims that emanate from any black body may be regarded as self-evidently true.

This is the racialized identity politics behind the students' demands—the *black body as an argument*. Unfortunately, there is nothing special about the black body. There is nothing special about any physical, racialized body, *per se*. Black skin does not convey the validity of an argument or a truth claim. It cannot justify a "themed engagement floor" because skin color does not represent a moral theme or any "theme," for that matter. Neither does white skin or yellow skin. Your body is not special until it conjoins itself to a mind and adapts nature to its needs, desires and rational aspirations, and its self-actualization and manifested agency. Any human body that merely weaponizes itself in a crudely racialized manner and fails to achieve a self-cultivated moral character that can communicate clearly in rational terms, with inscrutable and inexorable logic, is merely an ecological, social ballast—ignoble, exploitable, and a heap of unintelligible junk.

These students may have a safe haven while spineless university bureaucrats yield to their unintelligible shouts, snarls, moans, and groans. When they matriculate into the world with rational, practical, and reality-oriented people who wield unbending power and will not capitulate to their demands, reality, which ultimately cannot be cheated or faked, will set in. After having been given so many opportunities and the keys to heaven on earth in our great republic, they will eventually be tossed into the dustbin of history, screaming in abysmal terror at a universe that will care not one jot about them.

The anti-intellectualism of today's black segregationist students is a macrocosm of the intellectual health of our nation overall. But to use one's primordial and atavistic racial identity as a means of bartering for power is not pathetic or disgusting—it is tragic. This will not end well for the participants in this psychodrama.

It is sad because black students who attend the most accommodating universities that treat them both solicitously and with racial caution are fearful of white people, or they are tired of being around them. They are tired of the need they feel to perform before the eyes of white people who are always appraising black agency.

In the history of black/white relationships, black survival often meant passing the myriad of tests devised by whites to grant them opportunities, recognize their rights, and allow them to retain (if we think of the South) even a patina of their dignity.

But these are different times. This is a majority white country. By what mawkish fantasy do these snowflakes indulge to entertain a belief they deserve a luxury vacation away from white people? And by what lowly sense of appeasement and betrayal of rational principles would a weakened administration cower to such student demands?

There is also what I shall call *white embarrassment*. Guilt has tuned to embarrassment and, perhaps, in some cases, incredulity. Since the 1960s, whites have witnessed the spectacle of blacks declining academically. They are underperforming *vis-à-vis* all other ethnic and racial groups, regardless of socioeconomic status. Whites continue to watch as intelligence, articulacy, a disciplined work ethic, abstract thinking, and traits associated with genius are frowned upon by blacks as white attributes. They are embarrassed to see a people continue to atrophy in the school system, decade after decade.

Since progressivism had outlawed moral paternalism, they stood passively feeding the raging beasts rather than performing the endless task of every educational administrator and teacher, which is to humanize the beast, not placate it. Rather than cater to its feral nature, they should have cultivated its capabilities and pointed to its luminous potential. Rather than teach elocution in high school to blacks so they refrain from lauding Ebonics as the linguistic equivalent of English, they view any criticism of "black English" as racist. Unscientific machinations of linguists aside, any careful listener knows Ebonics is English laden with grammatical infelicities. It is time for blacks in America to stop sounding as if they are speaking English as a second or third language.

White university administrators have aided and abetted in the destruction of the black mind. They have done so by not defending the values of America and of Western civilization.

They have ceased to believe in those values as the proper birthright of all God's creatures. They have accepted the most racist of all educational ideologies, *multiculturalism*, which, among other things, promulgates the belief that persons coming from a distinct culture ought to be taught from their historical perspective, and that, according to Ibram X. Kendi, all cultures must be judged in relation to their own history. Our educative bodies, the majority of which are on the left-wing spectrum, have subscribed to the view that blacks are indeed human beings—just a different species in need of special educational needs!

By facilitating racially sensitive workshops, today's university administrators and corporate entities are in the business of cultivating *knowledge apartheid*. It is white progressives on campus and, by default, in business who are champions of the New Racists.

AFRO-PESSIMISM AND BLACK NIHILISM: THEIR DEATH WISH FOR WHITE AMERICANS

White professors in the humanities and social sciences, and the mostly white-led administrative bodies, are not on a suicide mission. They are looting cash cows who know that there is big money in social justice ideology and victim's identity advocacy studies. Suppression of free speech on campus by the cancel culture crowd, comprised of a large number of black students and their white counterparts, is tolerated. These white students are devoid of purpose; they are empty vassals who are spiritually bereft. Interestingly, they also are in search for whiteness and racial supremacy under the bewitching guise of abolishing whiteness.

This form of hypocrisy involved is one of hatred by ostensive oppression. If black victimologists hate America by virtue of their

153

suffering and historical exclusions from mainstream society, then these white left-wingers can gain street credibility by enlisting their black brothers- and sisters-in-hatred in solidarity. What the white bourgeois alt-left lack in personal oppression, they make up for in their righteous indignation over the plight of black victimization. Also, since black victims often claim they lack the institutional resources to showcase their suffering and perceived hopelessness to a large audience, what better way for white left-wingers to make themselves useful than by atoning for their social insignificance and irrelevance by creating a performance on behalf of the victims?

Our institutions of higher learning are largely, single-handedly devoted to the destruction of America—American values, reason, logic, objective values and, finally, Western civilization, which holds all such phenomena together. Systemic nihilism rules their hearts and minds as much as it ruled the semiliterate race hustling pimps of the 1960s who shuffled Black Studies programs together. That systemic nihilism also ruled the hearts of the New Negritudes, the black nihilists, and Afro-pessimists.

Today, cancel culture, black nihilism, Afro-pessimism, and calls for black separatism will eventually self-destruct. More on that later on. For now, we may say these pathologies stem from a black racial identity that was forged in the crucible of seventeenth to nineteenth century oppression, degradation, and exclusion. It was a stillborn identity, filled with notions of inferiority and inadequacy.

Self-confident, psychologically empowered and emboldened people do not remain enslaved for very long. The problem was not just the shackles and chains that had enslaved bodies—it was one of holding a premodern, tribal mind replete with a racial ideology that, when internalized, would map out the psychic life of black people for centuries ahead. It had a formula and a specious racial algorithm that would duplicate the same prototype of the racial black man and woman in perpetuity—talk of non-monolithicity among blacks notwithstanding. *Blackness* manufactured in the European imaginary would be proudly worn like self-made creations. Blacks wore the identities their masters imposed on them, rather than expurgating them once they were free.

This imposed racial identity came with an encoded script of inferiority, one constructed for exclusion and congenital idiocy. In the premodern white imaginary, the black person and his identity existed as a social problem, and he suffered from arrested emotional and cognitive development.

Yet, ironically, the emancipatory vocabularies of Western civilization and the universal middle-class values of the United States are often rejected by many black students today in favor of some unknowable, atavistic maintenance of their vestigial past—a past long lost in forest-clearings and villages decimated by untold diseases and lost cultures hundreds of years ago.

Behind the hoopla of black racial pride, many black people still carry the burden of that racial script; they still cling to a strong racial self-image. When that racial image-identity grafts itself onto an entire culture, its insignia is consumed by its members who, having been never offered an alternative to a poisoned racial identity, pretend it is a badge of honor.

I would submit that most feelings of inferiority and diminishment that blacks feel in the second decade of the twenty-first century come from the continued and internalized primordial identities inherited during slavery. Truly, they come from holding an archaic identity, replete with a psychological racial frame of reference, while trying to navigate an age of post-oppression.

This is not caused by trenchant racism in our country. To hold a strong racial identity like this is to sully oneself. It means that there are far too many blacks living tragically regressive and nostalgic lives. They are tethered to an unaltered past—the horrors of slavery. Many are unable to project a magnificent future they could command; they are grounded by ball and chain to a country they feel they do not belong because it has not responded to their desires. They are afflicted with chronic anxiety, fear, and an overwhelming emotion of needing to be something (a black person who performs in the world) versus being just a *person.*

To reveal the pessimism and nihilism at the hearts of so many blacks suffering internally under the accreted weight of black racial identities, we'll turn our attention to some of today's purported intellectual black nihilists and Afro-pessimists. It is easy to see how cryptically they write in depicting black nihilism and Afro-pessimism anthropologically. They seem, however, to embrace the descriptive markers of nihilism and pessimism into philosophic systems worthy of emulation.

In the end, as preconditions for the continued existence of black people, they advance the idea of the extinction of the white race. The abolition of "whiteness" they advocate is a metaphoric veneer that, when stripped back and analyzed, reveals not the relinquishment of the characteristics one would expect if one were trying to analyze the concept of "whiteness." The appointed, final resting place for the abolition of "whiteness" is death for white people.

The most ardent spokesperson for the philosophy of black nihilism, a staple of many Black Studies/Black Diasporic Studies programs, is Calvin L. Warren, a philosophy professor. Aside from lambasting the American Dream in a manner consistent with that of Cornel West, Ta-Nehisi Coates, and Nikole

Hannah-Jones, Warren gives both a quasi-normative account and a sociologically descriptive account of today's black psyche.

In his essay, "Black Nihilism and the Politics of Hope," he explains that black nihilism resists emancipatory rhetoric that assumes it is possible to purge anti-blackness. Black nihilism advocates *political apostasy.* It must also reject hope itself. Hope has to have politics to accompany it; black nihilism rejects politics and hope and a way of expressing that hope.

Warren states that the politics of hope must refuse the possibility that the "solution" is, in fact, another disguised form of the idea of a "solution," which is nothing more than the repletion and disavowal of the problem itself. The black self is an eternal problem because solutions cannot exist within the politics of hope, just the illusions of a different order in a future sense.

A refusal to do politics is equivalent to doing nothing. Nothingness is constructed as the antithesis of life, possibility, time, ethics, and morality. Ultimately, Warren concludes, "We must hope for the end of political hope."

Similarly, in his critically acclaimed book, *Afropessimism*, Frank B. Wilderson III notes that blackness is social death. It is never a source of plenitude, it is never equilibrium, and it is never a moment of social life. Afro-pessimism, he writes, is a looters creed; it is a critique without redemption or a vision of redress that can never come except at "the end of the world."

Implicitly indicting whites for the insolvability of the crises facing blacks, he notes that black bodies are a different kind of containment. They are threats to the human body ideal and to the psychic coherence of human life. His nihilism and pessimism are deep. He writes: "Blacks cannot say they are alike at a paradigmatic level; that I am truly a Human Being and not the other

157

thing…this cannot be guaranteed to the extent to which one can say: I am not Black."

The universe is metaphysically and invariably structured against blacks. All reality, according to *Afropessimism*, is a conspiratorial attack on blacks—not only must they deal with the terrorism of the police, the army, the prison-industrial complex, the mainstream media, the mega-church, and the universities, there is yet a third tier of terrorism against black humanity, an unrelenting terror that is elaborated whenever black people's so-called allies think aloud. They are the logic of feminism; the logic of working-class struggle; the logic of multicultural coalition; and the logic of immigrant rights. When these voices, often in the name of intersectionality, voice their grievances, they end up competing with black grievances—and all the members of the aforementioned groups constitute humanities against blacks. These third-tier terrorists scaffold the death of black desire. Through an interdiction against black performance coupled with a demand for it, we are guaranteed the erasure of blacks.

One cannot help but conjure up images of resentful blacks hating the spectacle of other beggars and sufferers who present their puss-filled sores for public inspection. The mere presence of these competing mendicants cancels out the existential significance of the black subject.

Deadly serious about how alone blacks feel in the world, Wilderson writes of competing minority groups signing their own theme songs: "Ain't Got No Green Card Blues," "Ain't Got No Same-Sex Wedding Blues," and "Ain't Got No Abortion Blues."

The tragic conclusion is that every rights claim made by a human rights group is an extreme mark for the exclusion against blacks. It further blots them out of existence. But it is a redemptive extinction. In Wilderson's view, blacks are condemned to be re-birthed for the perverse pleasures and repeated viewership of a sadomasochistic society. He writes: "Blacks won't be genocided like Native- Americans. We are being genocided, but genocided and regenerated because the spectacle of black deaths is essential to the mental health of the world. We cannot be wiped out com-pletely, because our deaths must be repeated visually."

Blacks, according to the philosophy of black nihilism and Afro-pessimism, occupy not just the least socially prestigious racial/ethnic identity, they are outside the realm of humanity. Humanity is the enemy. Wilderson writes: "Human Life (from which the black is exempt) is dependent on Black death for its ex-istence and for its conceptual coherence. There is no world with-out Blacks; yet there are no blacks who are in the world." In fact, outside the realm of salvation is the black body and soul: "The antagonist of the worker is the capitalist; the antagonist of Nature is the settler; the antagonist of the Black is the human being."

By "human being," he means white individuals.

His take on what he perceives to be the state of the current contemporary black imaginary is as follows: Blacks wallow in a problem that has no solution. Black suffering is that problem. Suffering without a solution is a hard thing to hold, especially if that suffering fuels the psychic health of the rest of the world. That's what it means to be a slave and host in a parasite called the Human (i.e., white people).

We must, therefore, surmise that if the slave is a host in a parasite called Human, then the slave is not a Human. It is something outside the sphere of humanity. It is a sentient, non-human being.

Wilderson sounds like he could be describing some image of how the European saw the indigene. He writes:

> "The black sentient is dead as human.
> The black as Human is non-living.
> The black as a member of a Race is,
> therefore, dead.
> So, it stands, there is no race. It, too, is Dead."

Afro-pessimism has no prescriptive gesture. The end of black suffering signals the end of the Human, and the latter is deemed as unethical. It is the parasite of the non-human black slave that makes regeneration impossible and life itself possible.

The nihilist and pessimist have declared war on all human beings who are not black, for they are then Human Beings apart from blacks. In stinging words, Wilderson writes: "The Human is unethical whether she is a communist, a feminist, a fascist, a misogynist. They are the embodiments of capacity. And for the Afro-pessimist, capacity is an offense."

Warren reminds us that the soul of black nihilism offers only philosophical death, as it reflects social decay. Black nihilism is a catalogue of dysfunctional behaviors. It is an "existential angst," a kind of collective *clinical depression*. It is a disease that resembles alcoholism and drug addiction. One can never be careful enough, as one is always susceptible to relapsing into the addiction.

Even the concept "meaning" translates into anti-blackness. Warren notes that for the black, *meaning* is lost. The black nihilist brings meaninglessness to the fore and discloses it in all its terroristic historicity.

One may reasonably conclude that, in the broadest of fundamental terms, the spectacle of Afro-pessimism and black nihilism are the apotheosis of racial narcissism. The racial self-absorption and the positing of it as an almost metaphysical axiom is a brazen attempt at immortality. The philosophy speaks of blacks not as a subject but as a void, a death. Yet it speaks; it is regenerative while living as death.

This racial narcissism is also idolatrous. It imagines that—in some post-theological conception of the political that is no longer rooted in sovereign glory and sacralized violence—it can supplant itself as a competitor religion.

And yet there is suffering. Not abject suffering, but real, bone-chilling suffering behind the jargon-infested philosophy that portends to speak for the collective psyche of black America. And to whom is the philosophy directed? Mainly, the Human Being. Humanity. The White Subject. To be more specific, the white man and woman.

The racial narcissism of this philosophy, were it not a cry of the heart and a plea for emancipation, would have remained silent. As mere observation, it would have no need to communicate the obvious to the rest of the dead black people outside the realm of Human Being.

And what is to be done? What are white people to do about the collective racial depression we hear experts on the black condition bemoan?

Undoubtedly, this malaise is traceable to slavery. "Post-Slavery Stress Disorder" is how some in the black community, who are subscribers to the black nihilist and Afro-pessimist philosophy, describe the source of their depression. If the already identified, concrete pathologies that mar black progress are reducible to Humanity—that is, white people's moral malfeasance—do

white people have a moral obligation to correct a structural problem they might have created?

If the scenario I painted above were true and demonstrable,
then an argument could be made for solutions. Black nihilism
and pessimism are not based on concretes, however. They are
floating abstractions with unsubstantiated claims tethered to no
empirical conditions of real people's lives. That is why its advocates reject emancipation, mitigation, and even help from others.
This would demand accountability and involve change. It would
demand that the philosophy ostensibly point out sociological issues that relate to black people and show how, in comprehensive
(and sometimes piecemeal or episodic) ways, tangible problems
could be solved.

But the advocates of this belief system cannot do this.

And white people (along with honest black folks) need to
pull the entire rug out from under these black race hustlers and
scammers who devise academic names to legitimize their moral
con games. Black nihilism and Afro-pessimism are intellectually
bankrupt and cannot be practiced consistently as a way of life.
White people should not capitulate to the guilt they are being
bullied into feeling, nor should they be hubristically seduced
into thinking they pull that much leverage over the lives of anyone—not even black people. Their attraction to this philosophy
is a form of narcissism. The system is really all about them and
the incredible power they have over black people. They have so
much power that they constitute the entire human project (the
Human Being) from which a debased, black non-human has
been historically excluded and is still excluded today.

The destiny of black people is not determined by the actions
of white people but by the values they hold, the character they
devise, and the ethos they carry into the world.

What has happened is that black identity was forged in the crucibles of oppression, racial injustice, humiliation, and unfreedom. Black bodies were still meditative sites of moral contemplation, moral ambiguity, and even of the immoral actions of racist whites. Blacks suffered—but they had *cosmic significance*. After the 1960s, blacks became like every other previously disenfranchised group freed and given full legal recognition. Nothing special. Ordinary. Average. No longer were their bodies deserving of moral, iconic status. They lost their *cosmic purpose*. This is the cultural-racial depression black writers speak about.

Cultural critic Ibram X. Kendi tells his black and progressive white readers and followers that black people are still living and dying in a slaveholder's republic. Kendi has written a bestselling book, *How to Be an Antiracist*, and he is the director for the Center for Antiracist research at Boston University. He is America's self-appointed racial expert who knows what it was like to hold racist assumptions, even about his own people. Now that he has been liberated by his own intrapsychic analysis of his once *verboten* moral conscience, his job is to teach white people that it is not enough to *not* be a racist—one has to be an anti-racist. This means committing oneself to policies that translate into racial equity and non-disparities between racial and ethnic groups, even when those disparities are not causally linked to racism.

Kendi is very serious about his racist anti-racist agenda. He writes: "The only remedy to racist discrimination is anti-racist discrimination. The only remedy to past discrimination is present discrimination. The only remedy to present discrimination is future discrimination."

Kendi, like other members of left-wing *Blackademia*, believes that racism is a constitutive and ineradicable feature of American life; the only alternative is to fight this intractable social affliction by applying more racial discrimination. This is simply a euphemistic manner of saying racism can only be fought by discriminating against white people through equity policies meant to guarantee absolute income equality between the races. This entails adopting policies that expropriate the wealth of whites and redistribute it to blacks who have not reached a level of economic parity with their white compatriots, regardless of whether such disparities are causally linked to racism.

The agenda here is open race war fancied up as policy-driven goals toward equity and fairness and a self-appointed, anti-racist guru who can alleviate white people of their inbred proclivities for racial prejudice, given the racially suffused society in which they were raised.

Kendi claims that he was born into racial puberty at seven when he entered an all-black school and encountered the only black teacher there. He demanded to know why she was the only black teacher; but she had had no answer. He concluded then and still concludes that it was a racial crime to be yourself. He declares that if you are not white in America, it is a racial crime to look like yourself or empower yourself. He also declared, by this reasoning, that he became a criminal at seven years old. Kendi would have found himself a criminal in 1989—a period in America's history when amnesty was being granted to thousands of illegal immigrants and wave after wave of Caribbean immigrants flooding the South and east coast. They found not intractable bigotry but streets lined with golden opportunities.

A careful reading of Kendi's book reveals a train of thought shared by today's leading black anti-American writers on the left, from Coates to Michael Eric Dyson. In their writings, the literal terrorization of their lives came from other black men, not from white people. All were subject to black terror and intimidation.

They point to the systemic racist institutions and the white supremacists' operative policies that create the deprived social conditions that produced the black thugs who harassed them during their childhood and adolescence.

Kendi is free to define himself as a criminal and implicitly indict white America for what he honestly believes is a correct self-diagnosis. This interpretational latitude is broad in the same manner as his ability to define words and create neologisms with such breadth and scope; he freely admits he does not believe in objectivity. Objectivity, he submits, is really "collective subjectivity." It is impossible to be objective; rather, he declares, we are required to tell the truth.

He is not deliberately intellectually out of focus. He knows that what he utters is unadulterated, pure nonsense. Truth is predicated on objectivity. Truths are determined from perceived facts of reality. Such facts much be discoverable in an objective universe that exists independently of human consciousness. These facts are unassailable and indubitable. Such is the nature of facts; they cannot change as a result of wishes and desires. When human consciousness perceives facts in reality, *truth* is the cognitive designation given to the codification of those facts.

Kendi gets away with conceptual inanities because he is a proud relativist. He prates endlessly that all cultures are equal and that differences are just that—differences with no qualitative distinctions affixed to them. He writes that all cultures must be judged in relation to their own history, and that all individuals and groups be judged in relation to their own cultural history and definition, not by the arbitrary standard of any single culture. This, he admits, is an expression of cultural relativity, which is the essence, he emphasizes, of anti-racism. To be anti-racist is to see all cultures in all their differences as at the same level—as equals. When we see cultural differences, we are seeing cultural difference. Nothing more. Nothing less, he declares.

Kendi's audience is white people, pure and simple. They are, in his world view, the ones who owe him and blacks anti-racist actions, policies, and the attendant result that must be forthcoming to prove one as an efficacious anti-racist. Unfortunately, what he has offered whites is not a manual or self-reflective account for how to become anti-racist but a method of disqualifying them from making any criticisms of black culture because they are non-credentialed outsiders and, therefore, at best, non-racist—which is not enough. To be a cultural relativist is not the equivalent of a non-confident seventeen-year-old who has not learned the art of moral reasoning. It is, in this case, an attempt to silence white people by telling them that if they see difference and attempt to affix a qualitative distinction to it, then they are racist. The twelve-year-old girl forced into child betrothal to a man four times her age, where she is raped against her will, or a five-year-old girl in Eastern Africa, forced to have her clitoris excised all in the name of cultural practices, are subjected not to violations of their bodily integrity, but to cultural practices in Kendi's worldview.

Kendi, though, is not alone. It is a common canard among the educated left-wing cognoscenti that all cultures are equal. Indeed, a few weeks after writing an article in which I declared that was not the case, the Acting Provost of DePaul University—where I am a tenured professor of philosophy—issued what I and many others considered to be a formal censure against me. She declared that it is considered an accepted truism that all *individuals are valued equally*, and that she was truly disheartened that a member of the academic community would assert that "not all cultures are indeed equal."

I had stated that some cultures are abysmally inferior and regressive based on their comprehensive philosophy and fundamental principles—or lack thereof—that guide or fail to protect the inalienable rights of their citizens.

Therein lay the category mistake that an educated academic along with countless others commit—conflating the individual with the cultural. A culture may be described as a multiplicity of complex systems that include the arts, laws, customs, practices, norms, mores, beliefs, knowledge, and capabilities acquired by human beings in society. Culture also includes language, ethical systems, and religious institutions. One can indeed say that all persons are endowed with equal and intrinsic moral worth as human beings, which they may corrupt by committing morally egregious acts; but as human beings, they are possessed of inviolable moral worth and dignity.

It is, however, a category mistake to transfer this innate respect and reverence for the individual onto the landscape of culture, which is not an indivisible whole, and possesses none of the requisite attributes of individuals that make them deserving of such unassailable respect. Persons' identities are not reducible to the practices of their cultures. Some cultural practices are downright horrific and evil; some are better than others. Persons in their respective cultures are free to identify themselves with those practices that align with their moral identities and distance themselves from those they find repulsive.

The Unites States is not a perfect civilization; however, as a rights-bearing culture in which the inalienability of rights is observed, a country in which civil liberties such as freedom of speech (for now) is still upheld, freedom of conscience and freedom of religious association (or lack thereof) is respected, it is vastly superior to barbaric and primitive cultures that have yet to discover the individual and his or her inviolate dignity. The United States is a republic devoted to the inalienability of those rights that are conducive to human survival and flourishing. The United States, through its Constitution and Bill of Rights, is the first political system to discover the direct correlation between the rational nature of *man qua man* and the exact political milieu in which that nature has to properly live and function *if* it is to live rather than perish.

Sudan, Nigeria, Mauritania, Libya, and Algeria—all countries which still practice and/or tolerate chattel slavery by Arab and black Muslims against other Muslims and Christians—are not the moral, political, or cultural equals of the United States, Israel, Great Britain, and France. Those countries are vastly superior to Saudi Arabia, Iran, North Korea, and Gaza, which do not permit religious reciprocity. Their political leaders allow the beheading of homosexuals in the streets, legalize torture, and have some of the most egregious records of gender inequality in the world. In the cases of Iran, Qatar, and Saudi Arabia, we witness them as sponsors of worldwide terrorism and of placing restrictions on civil liberties and a free press.

Cannibalistic Aztec culture could never and will never be the cultural equal of any civilized and free culture existing anywhere in the world today. Cultures that permit freedom of association, respect equality for all citizens and legal residents before the law, uphold gender equality, and allow individuals to cultivate their unique life plans are, generally speaking, cultures that have discovered that an environment in which freedom and liberty are *the* milieu in which the individual needs to cultivate his or her rational nature and live an optimal existence, are superior cultures, morally, spiritually, and politically speaking, to those that cultivate environments consonant with human nature, which require freedom and liberty.

It is a mark of sheer, cognitive malarkey to claim that all cultures are equal. Just as some cultures are technologically more advanced than others, so some are politically more distinguished in their record on individual rights and the protection of private property and personal liberties than others. Rape cultures—cultures in which rape is sanctioned by law such as in several parts of Pakistan and Afghanistan—are not moral equivalents of any Western democratic countries in which rape, though committed by moral deviants, is illegal and punishable by objective law.

Brunei practices a Sharia penal code under Islamic law that allows death or stoning for adultery, homosexuality, and even apostasy. Hamas continues to pose an existential threat to Israel by pounding the latter (unprovoked) with a barrage of deadly rockets so often that one can barely keep track of the attacks. It routinely arrests and tortures peaceful critics of its totalitarian government with impunity and is a blatant advocate and practitioner of jihadism. There is no culture, so to speak, inside Gaza. It is defined, incidentally, by its absence of any significant life and culture. Nevertheless, even countries that lack a significant culture can wreak havoc on the lives of others. A rich culture is potent because it creates life. One that is an ecological, sociopolitical ballast, or worse, evil, can destroy life.

The question remains of not only how to think about cultures that are unequal to others but what to do about those cultures that exist as rogue states and betray the civilizational maturity expected by an international order that protects the well-being of the global commons. We are talking here of morally inverted states that pose a serious threat to the international order—evil cultures that are political sinkholes that lie outside the process of history and are reverting to premodern ages. The goals of such cultures—among other things—are to eradicate the individual and practices of freedom and liberty.

Evil cultures are drainage systems that tax the existential, spiritual, and psychological resources of their citizens who must expend a disproportionate amount of energy just to stay alive—let alone flourish.

Let us rid ourselves of the simplistic, egalitarian idea that all cultures are equal. That some are moral and political sinkholes from which millions seek to flee is obvious. That such escapees or freedom seekers aspire to self-actualize in other cultures that, in their judgment, are better suited to their aspirations, hopes, and dreams, constitutes enough proof that some cultures are inimical to human well-being, and others are better suited for the development and practice of human agency.

What is Kendi afraid of? Why does he want to silence white voices? What is he afraid they might perceive, render judgment on, and pronounce a verdict about? It is black culture. Against the historic backdrop of black culture that was once so rich in literature, music, contributions in technology and engineering, dance and art, Kendi must admit that today's intellectual and cultural bankruptcy has bled into black culture as well.

Black culture today is dead. Against a forgotten panorama of black American culture rich in art/paintings, sculpture, literature, dance, music, technology and science, Kendi can only cite celebrated rap music replete with Ebonics, baggy jeans, dangling gold chains, piercings and tattoos, sexually boastful lyrics, and Timberland boots. These are the some of the artifacts of black culture he identifies in his books worthy of emulation.

Kendi, unlike Coates, is not ignorant of the historical achievements of blacks in this country. But he reduces black culture to the basest, most superficial level of caricature to establish how serious he is that even the lowliest qualifier for a cultural marker remains outside the judgmental ambit of the white, non-race-credentialed outsider. For him, differences are nothing more than differences. In Kendi's mind, an aping, crotch-grabbing rapper boasting about his "bitches" and elevating thug life and ghetto existence to an aspirational level is no different than Shakespeare, Homer, Tolstoy, or Madam C. J. Walker, the first black female self-made millionaire in America.

These gangster thugs are on equal footing with ex-slave Mary Ellen Pleasant, whose entrepreneurial holdings in the late nineteenth and early twentieth century were worth as much as $30 million at one time. Paul Cuffee, Anthony Johnson, William Ellison Jr., Antoine Dubuclet, Robert Gordon, Samuel T. Wilcox, William Alexander Leidesdorff Jr., James Forten, Amanda America Dickson, and Bridget Mason—all were slaves who became millionaires during slavery or in the aftermath of it. He does not mention Mary W. Jackson, the first black female engineer at NASA, or Katherine Johnson, a black female mathematician whose calculation of orbital mechanics as a NASA employee were critical to the first and subsequent US spaceflights. She played an unprecedented and historic role as the first black woman to work at NASA who mastered complex manual calculations and helped pioneer the use of computers to perform tasks associated with space travel.

Kendi cannot glorify the achievements of black individuals because the mediocrities he glorifies in those who are black would have to be judged by standards he regards as white!

For him, there is gender and sexual anti-racism and, finally, space racism. Space racism is a powerful collection of racist policies that lead to resource inequity between *racialized species* or the elimination of racialized spaces substantiated by racist ideas.

Space anti-racism is a powerful collection of anti-racist policies that lead to racial equity and integrated and protected racialized spaces.

We have gone from racist individuals to racist spaces and their antipodal counterparts. Kendi has charged the sociopolitical atmosphere with racist terminologies that, unproven, must be taken as having nothing to do with racial discrimination.

He believes all racial inequality is a direct result of racism, but this is simply untrue. There are fewer Asian players in the NFL and NBA than there are black players. This is not because Asian players are discriminated against or actively discouraged from these sports. For whatever reasons, blacks display a physical prowess that's challenging for another ethnoracial group to compete against.

This knowledge, however, does little to alter the consciousness of the civilizational nihilists who suffer from a willed civic and cultural illiteracy. From Greta Thunberg, nativists, white nationalists to black separatists and all racial and ethnonational particularists, woke fascists, and xenophobes of all stripes—the maniacal urge to fall into a state of wiled nihilism is deliberate, not accidental. The goals are to retrogress and reduce humanity to a state of premodernism. Their fear of independence, objective reality, and reason that care little for their mandates, cries of cultural appropriation, and marginalization, will be assuaged by an imagined community of individual silos that coexist, each with their own credentialed, tribal members, governing internal mores and protocols.

Kendi, and other black thinkers of the alt-left, make it abundantly clear that they would seek to immobilize a people's agency strictly by virtue of their racial identity. They are willing to target all institutions associated with white identity, even if it means bringing black people down with them. White identity and Western civilization are completely, inextricably linked for these thinkers. Whether it's Kendi's anti-racist, race rehabilitation centers, or Robin DiAngelo's racial sensitivity workshops (for mostly racist white people which is, by her definition, every white person born and socialized in racist America), white identity produces individualism and racial capitalism, all products of Western civilization and part of the "oppressive values of the Enlightenment project," in their view.

If white agency is constitutively constructed as racist for these individuals, then the concrete manifestations of that abstract agency shared by all whites must, for the non-racist, alt-left emancipators, be abolished. Those systems, for the new nihilists, are all oppressive, hierarchical, and exclusionary.

For Kendi, capitalism is not just the product of white agency; he believes passionately that to love capitalism is to love racism and that to love racism is to love capitalism. It is not my job to bog down the reader with the logical infelicities committed by this assertion, the paucity of reasoning exhibited, and the gross non sequiturs that follow from each of these utterances. It is not racial capitalism that he and his cohort of civilizational destroyers aim to abolish. There is no such thing as racial capitalism. It is a non-concept, which means it has no referent.

It is capitalism, individualism, reason, and personal responsibility they wish to annihilate and, worse, the capacity of each individual to be a transformative agent in his or her life without the help of a so-called enlightened racial guru to resocialize and rehabilitate persons from their racism. After inducing chronic guilt in whites, along with a chronic sense of hypervigilance that self-monitors their speech and actions in dealing with blacks, these anti-racist vultures stand ready to establish a "woke," left-wing, Marxist, totalitarian state. Western civilization and all its liberal principles of reason, sovereignty, freedom of expression, and conscience will have been criminalized. Annihilation of the individual—in this case, the annihilation of the white subject—is the goal of these power-lusters.

But what is the strange dance between the black annihilators, who advocate white annihilation, and their white counterparts, who seem to be advocating for their own destruction? Black nihilists live by some form of perverse, infantile, narcissistic fantasy that authentic black personhood can come only into existence when white people are extinguished while selling to idiotic white liberals the following idea: "No, what we mean for you to do is not kill yourselves off. We want you to abolish certain oppressive traits that are constitutive of your identity that we identify as fundamental characteristics of whiteness." These include: certainty, arrogance, defensiveness, and an unwillingness to be less ignorant, an unwillingness to break with apathy and white solidarity, an unwillingness to be humble, a capacity to believe any utterance by a black person that he or she feels is legitimate, using facts and logical argument to disqualify or invalidate the *feelings* of black people (who use their feelings as axiomatic truth claims that are above adjudication), and an inability to accept the primacy of feelings over rational thought.

Those liberal whites who play along with their so-called nihilistic black brothers and sisters in the call to abolish whiteness are of two kinds. The first feel there is a coming race war. They had better be on the right side of history, because when the screeching hordes of armed black mobs come hunting them like prey, they will have their race credentials in order and will be spared the march to the slaughterhouse.

The second type is more sinister, wiser, and more practical. They know that a white majority in this country will become a racial monolith and indiscriminately slaughter every black, gay, trans, and traitor to whiteness before they self-annihilate as a race. This group is the new liberal white supremacists who will wait in the shadows for the race war. Its members go along with blacks, playing the race card in every vulgar manner in which it can be showcased, all the while knowing there will be a white backlash against this moral malfeasance by black nihilists. The black victims will be in need of a managerial class and benevolent protectorates to champion and assure their continued safety.

Whiteness will be safeguarded and vouchsafed by a liberal, white supremacist class. They will have played the races against each other, and like a group of kids at a summer camp who drop a makeshift bomb in the latrine and then race away to watch from afar as everyone runs in panic from the crap exploding and showering them, they look at each other in bemused, ironic detachment and ask: "Wow, how did that happen?"

They are not good people. Their motives are evil.

The moral-political system of mutual exchange between consenting adults that has lifted millions out of abject poverty and physical depravity, decreased mortality rates, raised life expectancy, and is the only system consistent with human beings acting in their rational self-interest—capitalism—is cast as an evil offshoot of white agency. That this system has lifted blacks out of poverty and financed the educational systems that house people like Kendi, and the magazine Coates writes for is not lost upon them. They are entitled to a "payout" by a system they did not invent, which they claim continues to exploit them, while offering a deceptive facsimile of material success. That most blacks are not socialist or the enemies of capitalism is irrelevant to such nihilists.

They are part of a cultural Marxist cabal committed to destroying Western civilization by a combination of inducing guilt and granting credence and legitimacy to cultural and ethical relativism—thereby destroying not just the principles of correct thinking but, more narrowly, a method of human cognition that can discover, indubitably, the truth.

With human cognition arrested and the capacity to make qualitative discernments and secure judgments assured, starting in our universities—now indoctrination centers for anti-Americanism, anti-capitalism, reason, and freedom—the new systemic nihilists and new racial eugenicists can bleed Western civilization to death with thousands of tiny scratches.

After a global post-Marxist, anti-civilizational takeover, the final goal of the pessimists and the anti-capitalist, racial narcissists is to destroy human life as we've known it. They have not any thought of what they will replace it with, except ever-changing policies, whims, caprices, and cultural fads not founded in any moral or sociopolitical foundational reasoning or codified in law.

They have become environmental and political inverts who fear personal responsibility. They are possessed of a preternatural inability to navigate among the problems and tensions in the real world with reason and lucidity.

They are like incorrigible children, resisting the calls of maintaining a universal and emancipatory Western heritage where individual initiative and personal responsibility are required for personal success and civilizational upkeep. They simply want to be taken care of. They hoodwink a race of people into thinking that all cultures are equal, so that when individuals practicing inferior mores and customs fail because they adhere to them, they are absolved of responsibility; furthermore, they can blame the victimizing race for creating the conditions under which their challenged culture had to be compromised. Indeed, for a writer like Coates, gang members and black individuals who kill others, including blacks, are certified moral icons who deserve dispensation because, in his reasoning, they are powerless before the street crime of white history that brought the ghettos into existence.

The endgame of these players is extraction and extortion through moral sedition, induced guilt, and cognitive paralysis by educational balkanization. It's extortion via an appeal to helplessness and extortion for atonement because any sign of inequality of outcome between racial groups is a sure sign of virulent racism.

The new racial narcissists assume there is something special about the cosmic significance of blackness and about the black body. In attempting to hold the white imaginary hostage, they hold everyone hostage and shackle our civilization not to razed mountains but enshrined mediocrity. In a loud universal voice, we, the choosers of life and self-responsibility, ought to tell them to just grow up.

As mentioned previously, there is nothing special about the black body. There is nothing special about the physical, racialized body, per se. Black skin does not convey nobility. Neither does white skin or yellow skin. Your body is not special until it conjoins itself to a thinking mind and adapts nature and reality to its needs and rational aspirations, its self-actualization, and manifested agency. Any human body that fails to achieve a self-cultivated moral character and inscrutable human will is merely ecological, social ballas—ignoble, exploitable, and a heap of unintelligible junk.

FIVE

Should the Black Race Die So that the Individual Can Rise? The Heroic Race Traitor and the Road to a New Transracial Future

The fabricated black race should never have been born. It was artificially created out of false biological taxonomies by Europeans to justify a system of human physical bondage that paradoxically brought black people into the historical process. It was a cruel, artificial construct, and blacks have suffered enough under it. If racist whites owe blacks a reparative moral gesture, it is this—terminate your need to see blacks as blacks and refrain from establishing societal configurations that require them to prove their blackness. It is life-denying for blacks to resort to an appeal to their *blackness* as a legitimizing referent from which to both interpret and make sense of their humanity.

Such whites need to create no further factors or racial dynamics that will force aspiring moral, free black people to appeal to internal race consciousness to validate their lives and existence.

It is time to kill that racial ascriptive identity. Blacks have internalized an identity that was created for them. They were not any black people until the Europeans invented them. Like the homosexual who embraces the term "faggot" as a self-referential moniker and a legitimate referent that objectively refers to an objective phenomenon in the world—when, in reality, "faggot," is a non-concept and an empty set—so "black" as a racial category, used to designate any person with a patina of African ancestry in their blood, is a misapplied term.

What we seek is to develop an evolutionary paradigm from which the whole process of racism will end in a new planetary relation to freedom, defined by a transracial morality and benevolence extended to all persons in the name of a universally shared humanity.

Why have blacks so tenaciously clung to their bequeathed and inherited identities that were forcibly foisted upon them— identities manufactured to exclude them from the pantheon of the human community and the domain of the ethical? Why would any self-respecting black person proclaim racial pride in an identity that was branded on his back against his will any more than a cow or pig would showcase the brand stamped into his back to any of the other farm animals?

Autonomous, self-respecting persons do not proclaim racial pride when they originally had no race and were given an artificial one that eviscerated them of their dignity, self-esteem and, concomitantly, created conceptions of agency and personhood around those markers that branded them as biologically inferior and morally immature.

What self-respecting human being takes the master's naming authority over him and wears it proudly as a badge of honor, when the names affixed as racial monikers have changed at the whims and caprices of his master? Those named as black today have been called Negroes, quadroons, octoroons, niggers, colored, Afro-Americans, and African Americans. The black individual has been the subject of a reinvention more for white racist players than for any other group in the history of this country. The Irish, Germans, English, and Polish have been referred to by nothing other than what they have autonomously and independently named themselves as subjects—aside from pejorative slang terms. And such terms have been applied to every ethnic group in a vulgar, colloquial sense. They have never been used as constitutive identity markers for those groups.

Blacks have given up their sovereignty and autonomy in this respect. True, they have had no power to disambiguate themselves from what others with the powers to name them have chosen to call them. But I am referring to the zeal and passion with which they have internalized this racial identity as something precious and wonderful—as a mark of who they are authentically.

Not all blacks, it is true, hold to this strange self-hating form of self-identification. Many Caribbeans and Africans self-identify as black strategically, but internally, they refuse to hold a racial identity—one that forms part of their self-image. The idea to such individuals is unspeakable. Values, beliefs, and character are what constitute identity, not race, which is a neutral characteristic that reveals nothing about the core content of a person's moral agency.

Blacks remain atavistic racial determinists in their psychological makeup; they are mawkish sentimentalists attached to a fetishized history that forged an identity for them in the crucibles of horrific bondage. Their compromised imaginations simply cannot see where to go from here.

The 1964 Civil Rights Act should have been accompanied by a twin consciousness. First, to realize that, by the one-drop rule and by morphological markers that have been racialized, blacks marked as blacks would continue to be identified as such. Hence, a continuation of self-reference to themselves as blacks would be inevitable; it would remain the only viable way to redress future discrimination against them as black people. Second, they would have begun the process of deshackling themselves from an internal racial identity—the outward manifestation of which had been used as a legitimate insignia for legal persecution for centuries.

Deep introspection and moral reasoning inform one that race identity is an empty set—it is simply a sociological marker pretending to have moral and biological significance. One wins a war of discrimination via several means, which include certain virtues brought forth from one's moral character. Not one of those virtues has a racial hue to them.

In the name of a return to inviolable and inalienable individualism and self-respect, blacks ought to have made a vow to overthrow their inherited racial brand that has kept them tethered to a restricted agency. In the name of an intransigent individualism, we, the most raciated people on earth, will become a psychologically raceless people and open ourselves to the luminous potential of man and a new birth to the black individual as an individual.

A racial taxonomy that makes human distinctions not based on cultural differences, which can objectively be defined as the set of dominant beliefs, customs, and traditions of a homogenized or non-homogenized group, but based on race, which possesses none of the conceptual markers that allow us to predict or pick out any moral characteristic of a human being, is valorized by most blacks. The source of their oppression is worn fiercely as an honorific badge of racial authenticity. The white man called him Negro, black, nigger, colored—and he accepted it passively as his deserved birthmark.

To cling to a strong racial identity is a form of tribalism that is born of a deep narcissism where one needs to see oneself as special because of one's racial or ethnic identity. We frown upon homosexuality in many circles but accept *homoraciality* and *homoethnicity* as features of the natural world. We have weaned ourselves from our mothers' breasts, but we have substituted for the breast the name of the tribe, the race, the ethnos, and the *Volk*.

For black Americans, there is no real tribe or Volk. There are only long-deceased, imagined communities in Africa from which they have long been alienated and fantasies of an ancient Egyptian civilization few of them are tied to ancestrally.

Any black person who has ever suffered for his racial identity, and subsequently held on to "blackness" as a source of honor, has never been proud, never experienced self-esteem, never known what it was "to keep it real," never known genuine authenticity, autonomy, and sovereignty. Such persons have been the passive consumers of ready-made, secondhand identities tailor-made for them because they have never had the moral temerity to throw those identities in the faces of those who foisted them upon them and say, "We cannot refer to ourselves publicly any other way since the social reality you've created is so deeply entrenched, it almost operates with invariability, as do the laws of nature. But we will not internalize these identities as part of our self-identification. There is no pride in holding on to something you have used to oppress us. It is time for a race strike. No—it is time for us to be race traitors and make a new way."

To understand the morality of being a race traitor and the moral good that accompanies being one, I need to pose the question—is it even moral to hold and practice a racial identity? In my analysis, holding a racial identity and the relinquishment of it is an act of radical freedom. It is to position oneself in the world as a metaphysical rebel.

Let us begin the task of analyzing the moral status of holding internal racial identities as part of one's self-image. It is only then that we can explore the radically free metaphysical—the heroic, transracial race traitor who can usher in a new planetary ethic and give humanity an aspirational model on which to base his identity. What we shall call for is nothing short of the revocation of the black individual's membership in a race he never asked to belong to. The final restitution of the raceless community shall reside within himself. His own self-enclosure contains multitudes and is, itself, a disclosure of possibilities that race restricts and constrains. This is because racial identification as a moral self-marker is primordial and atavistic. When someone admits that he is a "race man," he is confessing his mummified state. He is bearing pride in being a hermetically sealed phenomenon, closed off from the world and from being affected by the encounters and exchanges with his fellow human beings. A "race man" is a deep misanthrope.

THE MORALITY OF HOLDING AN INTERNAL RACIAL IDENTITY

I think that holding a racial identity is problematic because it turns one into a practicing racist. On the surface this should not be controversial. White supremacists of all stripes, either of the North American variety or the Nazi counterpart, have given us ample evidence of the nefarious nature of strong racial identities, especially when they are wedded to a political ideology that demonizes racial/ethnic minorities such as blacks or Jews.

I am, however, going to go much farther in the scope of my argument to suggest that the concept of race, *simpliciter*, is bad. The concomitant practice of holding a racial identity voluntarily and living one's life as a raciated creature is a form of biological collectivism and racial subjectivism. It matters not whether one is black, white, Indian, or a member of any other designated group; the principle that binds all racial identities together—polylogism—is identical. To self-referentially hold a racial identity is to collude with a great social evil. This matters not if one is a member of a minority group (black) without the political means to institutionally discriminate on a large scale. It diminishes the scope of one's sociopolitical reach, not the fundamental nature of who one is. Thus, Cornel West is categorically wrong to argue, as he does, that *blackness* is an ethical identity.

Blackness is conceptually vacuous—it constitutes an empty set. Compared to *whiteness*—the practitioners of which have sociopolitical powers to enforce institutionalized racial discrimination—blacks who are racial practitioners become "petty racists" who, like the holders of all strong racial identities, are racial codependents. However, even those who attempt to make *whiteness* into a legitimate concept that designates specific attributes shared by all whites—short of the putatively obvious one which is skin color—have failed all meaning tests. Which is why the claim to abolish "whiteness" is really a euphemistic term meant to annihilate white people from the earth.

As an antidote, I shall posit the identity of the cosmopolitan transracialist as conceptually more robust. Its practitioners are imbued with moral traits and attributes that locate the constitutive features of the term and the identity of those who practice cosmopolitanism. The race traitor, the transracial cosmopolitan, is not just a lover of humanity. His identity is a moral competitor to racial identities, which, by nature, are exclusive and arbitrarily discriminatory. Cosmopolitanism is both a theory of the self and a robust moral system, replete with its own psychology. My goal is to argue that, aside from functioning as a more benevolent and humane way of existing with one's fellow human beings, the transracial cosmopolitan does the work of political advocacy in a far deeper and dignified manner than, say, any alleged ethical dimension of one who holds a racial identity. In short, transracial cosmopolitanism racially and ethnically cleanses the individual of the empirically untenable and largely imagined attributes one is deemed to have, and which, unfortunately, one has falsely adopted as a proper designator for who one is. Concomitantly, transracial cosmopolitanism corrects the empirically false beliefs that race consciousness generates about the moral and metaphysical status of individuals *because* of their racial identities.

RACIAL IDENTITIES

Racial markers are conceptually ambitious in that they purport to convey information about persons that, if taken seriously on the conceptual level, would yield necessary and sufficient conditions that all persons falling under a racial category would satisfy. The extant literature on why race fails as a biological category is already well-established and has, as far as I am concerned, concluded and won the debate over whether the taxonomies and racial classificatory schemas are empirically tenable. What survives in the public imaginary, however, are attributes that are taken to have moral salience, which are applicable to persons designated by historical and biologically fabricated markers. Sociological studies on the formation of European-American ethnic identities reveal a broad swath of traits that Europeans (some later designated as white) held about other groups believed to belong to different races. These traits—ranging from productive, smart, God-fearing, clean, and efficient to lazy, dirty, cognitively immature and irredeemably evil, were allocated among the various groups of raciated individuals with those assigned the most negative traits falling the lowest on the prestige index. Throughout the history of racial classifications in United States, to be black was to have the least prestigious identity.

A morally salient factor about holding a racial identity is that one must engage in affected ignorance or willed self-deception about oneself and about others. In the face of competing evidence, one holds certain views about oneself and about others that are causally linked to a form of racial subjectivism. The latter holds, among other things, that certain attributes one deems praiseworthy are laudable because one has them, and one has them because those attributes are causally primed by having the racial identity one has. The logical inverse of this form of reasoning is that if others have those attributes that are racially primed within themselves, they must have them incidentally, accidentally, do not have them at all or, at best, others have them imitatively. Whites, who hold a strong racial identity and predicate white superiority on advanced cognitive functioning that is treated as an irreducible primary because of its statistical consistency across a white population (especially when compared to the cognitive functioning of non-white populations), must engage in empirical obfuscation to maintain a psychologically consistent view of themselves over time. This self-cohesion depends on the willful distortion of the agency of others precisely because of imagined attributes the demoted group has that the superior group cannot logically have. The inverted reasoning of whites who hold a strong racial identity would seek to identify those who lack advanced mental functioning as simply a failure to exercise an innate potentiality within them. At the same time, blacks who display cognitive superiority are merely aping the behavior of whites in whose image they have fashioned themselves. This is what is called "white normativity."

But the moral ambitiousness of racial designators is not to be found in the attempts of its users to function like epistemological and conceptual wholesalers in the realm of locating moral agency within racial registers. No robust theoretical claims can be made about moral attributes if they are indexed to racial identities. The moral ambitiousness of those who utilize racial designators involves bypassing the claim of empirical untenability on the individual level, i.e., that some members of the demoted race are, in fact, better or smarter than they are. That certain members of the alleged superior groups are cognitively inferior and certain members of designated inferior groups have cognitively superior members becomes irrelevant. The racially and morally ambitious practitioners disambiguate the individual from his own cognitive register and wed his overall moral efficacy and superior status to his *associative relationship* to the group. A moron in the alleged superior group is not only less of a moron but, speaking in terms of the aggregate, he is not a moron, since his character is appraised against the highest denominator or normative features in his group. The essential defining characteristic of his group is predicated on superiority—genius, articulacy, productiveness, cleanliness, and efficiency. Inversely, the cognitively superior person in the low prestige group is always adjudged by the lowest common denominator in that group, which is taken as the definitive feature that he and all members intrinsically hold, despite individual exceptions, such as himself. Nothing in human reality could explain why, for example, the English held steadfastly to the view that a colonial subject, regardless of how well he mastered the Queen's language, how respectably he comported himself, how impeccably he dressed, and how he executed the most exquisite manners in the public sphere, could never become English. A colonial subject could never be an English man, and the same fact held for women.

Holding a racial identity voluntarily, it turns out, is problematic not just because of the false beliefs on which it is predicated. Those holding racial identities who exercise state institutional power can and have caused great harm. There is no need to revisit that argument, as it is pretty old hat. What makes holding a racial identity highly problematic is that it is a form of *biological collectivism*.

Biological collectivism is not a variant of racism as much as it is a species of tribalism of which racism is simply a concrete manifestation. Any attempt to identify a human being in morally significant ways based on his or her genetic lineage was bound to be a form of evil, even if it falsely ascribed positive traits to a group without the concomitant damage to another group. It would be an evil because the individual willfully commits an error of evasion. In doing so, he fails to properly distinguish himself from animals by invalidating the specific attribute which distinguishes him from all other living species—his rational faculty. One chooses chemical predestination, a form not just of biological collectivism but of abject mysticism over individualism and ascription over achievement.

As Ayn Rand famously articulated, racism is a crude form of biological collectivism largely because the appeal to innate ideas which form the racial template of persons living according to racial ideology betray free will. As a result, this appeal to innatism violates the concept of the individual as volitional, one who is morally responsible for the creation of his or her virtues. Those who seek their deepest sense of identity from race approach the subject of virtue as if it were an inheritable trait.

The reduction to animality is not what I believe is inherently objectionable in racist ideology, nor even the violation of the principle of individualism. One need not be a racist to commit any of those tenets. Indeed, one could be an economic collectivist and still—albeit in a difficult way—honor the individuality of another person. One would commit serious breaches of logic along the way, but we can still imagine a socialist adhering to individual rights in the realm of bodily integrity and freedom of speech—perhaps in a curtailed manner.

But racism not only eviscerates one of total dignity; it also ascribes moral responsibility to imputed characterological traits (good and bad ones alike) largely because one is believed to have inherited them. It is bad because it is one of the lowest forms of irrationality one can descend into—it makes irreversible the idea of inherited vice and discounts virtue in the person who has cultivated it on his own but whose ancestors are given credit for the moral achievement. Both deprive the individual of the exercise of reason. The inalterability of character traits through blood is established as ideal—one gets in life what one deserves through the mystical mixture of blood and body fluids.

This biological collectivism that allows individuals to be judged not by their characters but by the codified character traits and actions of a collective of ancestors, which approximates some vague, undefinable ideal, trades on associative identification as a shortcut for earning and arduously maintaining a moral identity as an individual. To be a biological collectivist means that one rides on the prestige value of one's racial identity, suffused with the moral attributes of everyone but oneself. In this sense, holding a racial identity means that one is morally lazy.

Inversely, those who hold strong racial identities make individuals into biological collectivists by judging them according to a racially subjective algorithm whose formulae are the actions and attitudes of others who are codified and given a racial denotation. This racial denotation becomes a metaphysical template that is the foundation of all racial stereotypes.

To exercise moral laziness, regardless of whether one holds a view that one has duties to oneself, is condemnable to the extent that such laziness implicates others, condemns them, and relegates them to oppressive modes of existence. One could argue that moral laziness resulting in intermittent failures to cultivate the moral traits or virtues such as honesty, benevolence, a propensity for promise-keeping, and fairness may not be condemnatory. Given, however, that most, if not all, moral traits and virtues are relational and do affect other people's lives, it is difficult to imagine how moral laziness could ever not affect others negatively. Moral laziness that is the direct result of holding a racial identity and stems from a race consciousness that generates false beliefs is philosophically indefensible.

What makes holding a racial identity in the cultural or biological sense morally problematic is that one makes not just a shortcut to achieving a moral character. Instead, one engages in the appropriation of characterological traits of one's ancestors and relies on a specious form of chemical predestination and associative identification to cultivate a sense of self-esteem and moral self-worth. The moral untenability of holding a racial identity is brought into sharper relief if we go beyond the fact that it breeds a form of moral laziness because it disincentivizes one from creating an individually constructed moral identity by riding on the social prestige of one's ancestors and deriving self-esteem and moral status from associative affinity. This, as we have seen, arises simultaneously from psychologically and existentially attenuating the agency of those outside the sphere of the extolled group for the enhancement of one's racial prestige. Moral laziness is a direct corollary of the act of valorizing ascription over achievement.

RACIAL SUBJECTIVISM AND POLYLOGISM

Let us consider a deeper question of why holding a racial identity is ethically untenable. To do so, we will revisit the two concepts on which all racial identities are predicated that we discussed in the previous chapter—racial subjectivism and polylogism.

All holders of racial identities are racial subjectivists and polylogists. These two character markers are so egregiously wrong and harmful—to oneself and others—that to adhere to the structures of thought that inform them is to engage in massive character distortion.

Racial subjectivism holds that an individual's inborn racial constitution determines his mental processes, his intellectual outlook, his feelings, his thought patterns, and his conclusions. Such conclusions are held to be valid only for the members of a given race, all of whom share the identical underlying constitution.

Nazi theorists claimed that knowledge and truth were peculiarities that originated in specific forms of consciousness and are aligned exclusively with the essence of their "father consciousness." What is presupposed here is an unbridgeable, epistemological gulf that separates human beings of different races and prevents peaceful conflict resolution.

Holding a racial identity is not only morally compromising but also misanthropic, since it introduces a gulf between the humanity of oneself and those outside of one's group based on speciously formulated and arbitrary racial taxonomies that determine ascriptive racial identity. The adoption of a racial marker, the moral grammar of which is hinged to the denigration of outsiders and "necessary illusions" about the allocation of ethical attributes among persons of the world, is the voluntary adoption of an irrational form of discriminating among human beings. This is self-evident. What is not self-evident is that the misanthropy is the expression of an act that once executed becomes almost irreversible—recusing oneself from a significant segment of the human population for reasons that are morally irrelevant.

Recusing oneself from the human project is in and of itself not necessarily immoral. Suicides do just this, as do hermits and recluses. And while a rational case can be made for suicide or living as a hermit, one is hard-pressed to see how racial recusal can have an ethical dimension. The racial misanthrope who recuses himself from the human project establishes a new humanity, one that is idolatrous, narcissistic and fashioned in his own image, replete with all the normative attributes he reserves for himself and his kind. These are attributes that others, by virtue of their racially essentialized identities, can never acquire. Peoplehood is a brute axiom regarded as invariable as the laws of nature. It is not an aspiration based on moral and political principles.

Those outside the pantheon of the racial misanthrope's highly artificial world are also, in a strong sense, outside the domain of the ethical. Since race in the biological sense has already been disproved, a belief in race is tantamount to a belief in elves, fairies, and winged horses. A socially constructed belief in race runs the risk of implicating one in psychologically investing that race (in and of itself). Whether socially constructed or biologically posited, racial attributes are almost always reified in the consciousness of those who invest in them and/or hold them. In this sense, they have a biological connotation in the minds of their practitioners and, because of this, holding a racial identity almost always permits some degree of psychosis.

There is, however, another sense in which it is believed that holding a racial identity can be ethical. When one holds a racial identity and uses it as a form of political advocacy rather than, say, a cultural identity that promotes a sense of racial particularism, then one can ethically hold the identity. Thinkers such as Alain Locke and Cornel West have advocated this notion, and West goes further in arguing that blackness can be viewed as an ethical construct. He notes that blackness has no meaning outside of a system of race-conscious people and practices. Being black within the context of historical abuse and degradation means being minimally subject to white supremacist abuse and a member of a rich culture and community that has fought such abuse.

West's attempts to classify "blackness" as a competitor term to the historical one that equated it with inferiority and a phalanx of negative attributes that stripped black people of dignity and agency is understandable. Blackness, however, once it is recused from its racist and racialized definition, one that falsely constructed it along the inferior axis of human agency, is an empty set—a non-concept. It is a non-concept because it cannot securely codify the necessary and sufficient characteristics that would allow us to signify "blackness" in a way that would designate an unqualifiable attribute pertaining to all black people.

When we think of terms such as "generosity," "braveness," "sarcasm," or "narcissism," we think in terms of fundamental attributes that give the terms their identities and which squarely denote the behaviors to whom the terms apply. It would be ludicrous to refer to a person who freely gives of her time and money to sundry causes as "miserly." The point is that "blackness" is conjoined to a person who exhibits a plethora of behavioral traits, from hooliganism to sophistication and dignity. There are no fixed behavioral traits that we find among blacks that singularly apply to all black individuals. No leader of a disenfranchised group—be he Martin Luther King Jr., Mahatma Gandhi, or Nelson Mandela—has ever fought injustice from either a racial identity or by appealing to a core dimension of the racialized identity as a basis for advocacy. King, Mandela, and Gandhi all used universal moral vocabularies that circumvented the appeal to standpoint particularity. King appealed equally to Vietnam War veterans as he did to the poor of all races and social classes. His racial identity was incidental, a sociological platform for advocacy, but not an existential grounding for rights and social and political enfranchisement as used by a garden-variety of black nationalists.

Since blackness is a non-concept and cannot be conceptually distinguished from the behavior of the lowest common denominator of its adherents any more than it can from its most ethically exalted, the term itself should be dropped from the social imaginary. It gives us an approximate understanding but refers to literally *no-thing* in reality. It is, in effect, a floating abstraction—that is, a concept that is bandied about with no specific referent to any tangible object, under which is subsumed no specific units that tie the concept into a coherent and metaphysically perceivable existent.

Those who use the term "blackness" to gauge the ethical status of those identified as black are left conceptually out of focus when the term is also used to describe ethically transgressive behaviors of individuals who apply the term to themselves.

And it is this that proves the untenability of attempting to use racial terms in definitional senses. If race is an arbitrary and metaphysically illicit construct, then there can be no manner in which a subsidiary term such as, "blackness" can lead to anything but conceptual indistinctness and, *a fortiori,* cognitive confusion. Blackness is not an ethical identity. It is, as I have stated, an empty set.

While I remain a firm opponent of multiculturalism and adversary of the racial politics of identity, I do not believe that all forms of identity politics stem from nefarious motives. In the case of the identity politics of, for example, Cornel West—of whom I am not an admirer—I believe it comes from a place of deep moral wounds and from a lifetime of having one's dignity eviscerated by both governmental and private racism. It is not, I believe, sufficient to say that no person of self-esteem will be harmed by racism because racism is a form of psychosis. When inflicted on children at an early age, if there is no philosophy of individualism available to them against which they can seek moral and philosophical redress, the damage is incalculable.

Private individuals may have the legal right to be racists, but they are just as heinous and morally reprehensible as state racists. One may uphold their legal rights while damning, in categorical language, the immoral audacity with which they wield their private racism.

Nowhere is this more evident in the actions of individualists who, rather than damn any racist, spend more of their time defending the restaurant owner who hates Jews and blacks and refuses to serve them. I respect the legal right of the businessman to treat his business as an extension of his home and indulge in racist discrimination. However, I find it difficult to expend more energy regarding him as a hero or to defend his right to "private" discrimination than I do his retention of racist attitudes in the first place. Legality may supersede morality in places where one has the legal right to be immoral if one is not violating the rights of others. Yet the moral harm that remains in place when individualists fail to do their homework adequately is astounding. It seems that one can defend the legal right of the racist businessman while telling him what he is—an immoral lout! In the moral division of labor, both jobs can be performed simultaneously.

TRANSRACIAL IDENTITY AND INDIVIDUALISM

There is a successor term that does the ethical work of advocacy for those disenfranchised by markers of race and class, sexual orientation, religious affiliation, and gender. Not only is the term a wholesaler in the realm of the moral work it does on behalf of representing seemingly disparate groups of people who are unjustly treated, it is also a viable replacer for racial identities. Unlike holders of racial identities, the *transracial cosmopolitan* is both the possessor of a distinct self with a unique moral psychology and the holder of an identity suffused with real attributes.

Cosmopolitanism is not just a sentiment or a perspective as many thinkers have made it out to be. It is both a moral system and a theory of the self that can provide authentic answers to probing issues in the contemporary era. In its strong form, cosmopolitanism becomes a moral and intellectual system to contend with. It debunks the shibboleths of group solidarity by demystifying the selective and arbitrary criteria on which group identity rests. It is highly individualistic in form, and its proponents argue that only individual persons—not cultures, races, or ethnic groups—are the bearers of rights and the possessors of an inviolable status worthy of respect.

As a philosophical movement with historical roots in the Cynic and Stoic philosophical traditions, cosmopolitanism has championed the inviolable dignity of each individual and posited that each person (not group) be a unit of ethical concern. The core notion of cosmopolitanism is that one's identity is not determined solely nor primarily by any racial, national, or ethnic background. A cosmopolitan is an individual who disavows all partisanship and parochial commitments of localities, city-states, and principalities.

Diogenes and the ancient Cynics began the cosmopolitan tradition by forming the notion that an individual could have a primary identity apart from the one he or she inherited from the polis. In de-emphasizing the values of class, status, national origin, and gender, the Cynics simultaneously placed great emphasis on reason and moral purpose. Here is the revolutionary idea that the Cynics achieved, which is a given in the Western concept of personality and its concomitant dependence on dignity—regardless of how much one is deprived of the concrete goods that are constitutive of social identity, one possesses a larger universal identity grounded in reason, moral purpose, and, above all, human dignity. Today, when contemporary cosmopolitans speak in terms of a universal human identity that they share with others, they are invoking concepts bequeathed to them by the ancient Cynics.

The concept of world citizenship, in the sense of belonging to all of humankind, gained ascendancy in the Hellenistic era. It is among the core features of Stoic thought, which, along with its great rival Epicureanism, were reactions to the gradual disappearance of the small city-state in an age of empire. (One of the reasons for the current upsurge in interest in cosmopolitanism is our own relation to empire.) As Philip of Macedonia and his son, Alexander the Great, imposed an overarching monarchy on the Greeks and conquered new territories, not only did the *polis* cease to be the sole seat of political authority for citizens, but they were also no longer insular safe havens in which local identities could be formed.

The *cosmopolis*, that vastly growing space beyond the insular *polis*, the place that, heretofore, had been the home of barbarians, was conceived of as a place where social and cultural distinctions were irrelevant compared to an essential sameness to all human beings who were bound together, regardless of their backgrounds, by their subjection to natural law. Human beings may live in a multiplicity of ways, but there is a law that holds the variations in their actions and behaviors to a recognizably human model. The people in one village may live in an area populated with plants, some of which are poisonous and some of which are not; those of another may live off the meat of animals. In the first scenario, someone must learn how to detoxify plants and classify them and establish that as an art or science. In the second scenario, one may establish procedures for effective hunting. In both cases, everyone must live by the evidence of his or her senses and experiences. That is what is to be expected, since human beings are conceptual animals; this shared nature provides the basis for a universal humanity. So goes the reasoning of the Stoics.

A contemporary cosmopolitan would point out that in no culture would you find mothers arbitrarily offering up their young to strangers, that individuals in all cultures have capacities for responding to shame and loss of dignity, that ethical human beings in every culture historically have condemned incest and rape, and that such examples are just a few among several that are the shared core features that all human beings have and that override local particularity.

Cosmopolitanism stands in contrast to multiculturalism and pluralism. Pluralists defend the view that individual identity is to be configured within the parameters of a conceptually neat ethnic, national, or racial paradigmatic prism. Pluralists are not separatists, but they do insist that the boundaries that make separate identities distinct (Italian, German, Native American, for example) are protected and kept in place. Group solidarity and identity, then, are the important values upheld by those in the pluralist camp.

Cosmopolitans, in keeping with the pro-individual stance first evinced by Diogenes, are of the view that human socialization takes place in the world where human intercourse takes place—in the multiple spaces that we inhabit and among the myriad human beings with whom we interact and exchange stories, experiences, values, and norms. Strong cosmopolitans repudiate the tendencies of cultural nationalists and racial ideologists to impute moral value to morally neutral features, such as skin pigmentation, national origin, and ethnic background. They argue that there is no one fundamental culture to which any individual is biologically constituted and leaves the question of identity entirely to the individual. Individuals ought to be able to cull their own identities based on the extent to which their experiences and life roles have allowed them to be the persons they take themselves to be, instead of the passive wearers of tribal labels assigned to them by their culture or by the society at large.

In keeping with their dignitarian stance, cosmopolitans are more egalitarian than those with racial identities who, however benignly, still discriminate based on constructed racial attributes. They assume that all persons, regardless of racial identities, have intrinsic and equal moral worth, and they allocate equal moral attention to all persons who have equivalent standing in the domain of the ethical. All "races" and persons belonging to those fabricated racial groups have equal standing. All individuals are treated as individuals who, incidentally, belong to contrived racial groups. Because groups as such have no primacy within the cosmopolitan world view, it is the inviolable worth of the individual that is extolled. As such, there can be, under the cosmopolitan morality, no search for social prestige, glory, and psychological well-being via an appeal to racial membership in a community. Strong cosmopolitans would frown upon such a goal for the simple reason that it is a form of moral appropriation or theft. The moral and existential endowments and achievements of individual members of a racial group are the property and achievements of the individuals who have created them.

I hope that the case against the holders of racial identities, whether they be German Aryans, black, Hindu nationalists, or Native American tribal leaders who claim ancestral rights to the artworks of their tribal members, can be understood more clearly. Riding on the prestige of the moral and existential endowments of a fellow racial tribesman is, as I have argued, morally lazy, a form of appropriation and, I might add, indicative of a gross deficiency in self-esteem and self-respect. No self-respecting person of any "race" will attempt to make himself feel better by riding on the largesse of a fellow racial member.

The moral transracial cosmopolitan would simply feel inspired that someone from the human community has made it possible for him or her to aspire to greater heights by demonstrating that human greatness and achievements are possible. The cosmopolitan's strength lies in the fact that no group or its members assume a greater share in humanity than any other.

Cosmopolitanism, racially and ethnically, cleanses the individual of a false identity that was constructed, in the case of blacks, to denigrate them. In the long run, such identities, I believe, are psychologically untenable and existentially and empirically false. The construction of race—the great ecological disaster of the modern world—has inflicted so many human casualties and moral harm that whether one relies on a racial identity to feel a sense of belonging or a misguided sense of false pride from holding such an identity becomes irrelevant. I submit that any ethically-minded person who holds a strong racial identity ought to strategically give it up out of recognition that racial worlds are, inevitably, warring worlds.

Strong transracial cosmopolitans have, as their goal, the complete *deracination* of peoples of the world—in the psychological and moral sense of the word.

Suffice it to say that strong racialists suffer from the metaphysical concomitant of any variant of biological collectivism and its existential corollary, *tribalism*, which manifests itself in an inability to create a moral and independent identity of their own, separate and apart from the codified record of their ancestors and current racial compatriots. Here, we find racial narcissists who need to see individuals who look like them reflected in the realm of their values; they suffer from a chronic inability to stand on them without the buoyancy of "racial uplift." The holder of a racial identity is, therefore, not so much immoral as he is mired in a form of psychic infantilism. He is unwilling or unable to matriculate outside the protective patronage of the tribe, and as such, remains cognitively in a state of arrested development. He is an unfortunate simulacrum of the original image of those who had constructed him as the racial archetype he spent his life rejecting or, as in the case of a racial majority that constitutes itself as the normative standpoint of human aspiration, he is a bloated caricature without personal worth or value.

THE BLACK INDIVIDUAL AS BEST SUITED TO BE THE HEROIC TRANSRACIAL RACE TRAITOR

Most black people reading this book will take umbrage at the suggestion that they should relinquish their internal identification with race. Most will find the normative command to be a race traitor as scandalous. The reasons are understandable; they have been socialized to be race creatures. It would be as ludicrous to ask them to stop speaking in English and to learn some foreign language not associated with their upbringing. The difference, though, is that while being branded with the imprimatur of blackness may not have damaged each black person equally, it was never devised to enhance the quality of life of any living black person. It was devised as a derogatory and degrading identity by white Europeans, and it remains constitutive of one's agency. It was not an accident of birth. It was a social invention created by those in power to stifle the agency of what is, by nature at birth, a blank slate. Race and its forced imposition on a people are corporeal colonization. It is atavistic and dated.

Wherein lies the pride?

How can one be authentically proud to be something that was created in one as a negative and to consciously denote an absence of one's humanity?

Blacks, to this day, complain bitterly that their racial identities, which were imposed on them, are used by whites to hold them back in life as a source of discrimination. Yet, paradoxically, they proclaim love of that identity and cherish the source of the anguish they believe their oppression comes from.

I believe backs folks cannot continue to have it both ways. Black cultural depression is drawn at the fault line of this logical contradiction. Like a battered wife loving her abusive husband and justifying the love by pointing to the ways the abuses are proof of his responsiveness to her—therefore, she must be alive—blacks are in love—for all their protestations—with their abusers and the object of that abuse—racial identity. So low is collective black self-esteem that they continue to be the downtrodden legatees of a racial identity they internalize that (in their minds) penalizes their humanity to the core. Yet they protect its authenticity and purity as if it were something crafted by God himself and as if it were an immutable law of nature without which their lives would be compromised.

Therefore, more than any other racialized group, black Americans are ideal candidates for *racial self-emancipation*. This will not mean that they will cease referring to themselves as black. The world at large, as I have said, has picked out morphological markers and racialized them. In a very real way, people of color are stuck with those designators. But they can cease identifying psychologically and morally with the burdensome evil of racial ascription and all the ways in which it circumscribes life.

They would do well to follow the example of Africans. In thirty-five years of living in America, I have never once heard an African refer to him or herself as black. They use a national, ethnic, or regional affiliative designator to make partial sense of who they are.

Black Americans may learn the process of decoupling their robust or even surface self-images and depth-identities from racial-inflicted, denigrating identities designed for them for myriad reasons. As I have explained, race is grossly limiting psychologically. It involves a script replete with imagined communities, artificially created people, and it posits a fate and destiny beyond which no one ought to aspire. It is true that, today, in terms of achieving one's life goals, race is no longer a chief determinant of destiny. But it is a psychological barrier in the nefarious ways in which internalized identity politics plays out in the consciousness of many black people. Ways of being in the world are circumscribed; habits around cultures and ideas are dictated by the racial script which others unquestioningly accept as their own personal narrative.

Racial consciousness is stultifying. Blacks achieved emancipation from slavery in the nineteenth century and legal freedom in the twentieth century, but they are still clinging masochistically to a dated and rancid eighteenth century European coinage which they ought to have outgrown by now.

Afro-pessimism and black nihilism still show the addiction most blacks have to white conceptions of black agency. "Whiteness" is a non-concept, an empty set like blackness. As we have witnessed, the lugubrious cries of the heart to abolish whiteness accompanied by desperate attempts to shore it up as a legitimate concept with defining attributes and distinguishing characteristics betrays a homicidal, infantile wish-fantasy for the genocide of all white people form the earth. As if the death of white bodies will cleanse the raciated black imaginary of the putrefied shame and guilt that accompanies a tarnished, strong racial identity that suffuses race consciousness.

The oppressed black racial trope has been one of the greatest aesthetic grotesqueries and moral transgressions emblazoned across the universal sky of humankind in so histrionic a manner that it, at times, threatens to rival the Holocaust. Like invidious beggars comparing their sores for proof of degeneration in black suffering and the harm done to black agency, many blacks hold up their historically scarred bodies like religious icons; they are objects whose suffering was not just based on racial injustice but on something like a cosmic malfunction—a metaphysical misordering of man's place in the universe. That suffering is taken as the paradigmatic, unalterable suffering, as has only been experienced by black people.

EXAMINING THE PROFILE OF THE NONRACIAL INDIVIDUALIST

Today, official names for complex persons with modes for superlative evolution do not really exist. We are unable to formally distinguish extraordinary, norm-shattering individuals from those who do not contribute anything to the future. They simply condemn life itself to entropy.

Karl Jaspers wrote: "The human being is an open possibility, incomplete and incomprehensible. Hence it is always more and other than what he has brought to realization in himself."

White Europeans built a racial paradigm, and blacks guarded it in their souls with an addictive and mystical fervor. All sorts of mythologies, false narratives and imagined communities were summoned by the black imaginary to dignify that identity.

We may liken black identity to the psychological equivalent of Stockholm syndrome. Not only have blacks internalized a degraded racial identity foisted upon them, but, in their minds, the white "oppressor" lives simultaneously alongside it. Black identity can never truly be free; in that identity, the white individual and his or her identity is a constitutive feature.

The Afro-pessimists and black nihilists conjure up a perverse fantasy that, for the creatively unimaginative and inefficacious, would result in a truism—if all the white people disappeared today, the black race would cease to exist, and thus, blacks would be free on all fronts.

But contrary to the sadomasochistic death wishes of the black nihilists, white people are not going anywhere—nor should they. Whites have every right to exercise their privilege, as do the educated, the athletically superior, and the emotionally intelligent.

The transracial cosmopolitan, like all of us, uses the transcendent component of his personality, his not-yet-self—that aspirational part of himself that covets a future that will be created out of the limitless possibilities for life he carries in his being.

The transracial race traitor is what we may term an event-making individual, a social disruptor, and existential game changer. Eventually, he redetermines the course of history by altering human consciousness along an evolutionary path. He perceives the deepest anatomical and genetic structure of black racial identity. He sees that it was forged in the crucible of contempt and degradation. He identifies the zoomorphic and bestial nature of it from its inception and the qualities of inferiority associated with it. He sees the lies on which it and all racial identities are predicated.

In the spirit of Jewish theologian and philosopher Abraham Heschel's distinction between *process* and *event*, our transracial hero intuits that he has been living life as a process herd creature. A process is a phenomenon that happens regularly; it follows a basic permanent pattern. An event is extraordinary, irregular. A process can be continuous, steady, and uniform. Events, however, happen only intermittently and occasionally; they are engineered by rare phenomena. To live as a process person is to be typical; to live as an *event* person is to live as a unique being. Nature is comprised of processes in the form of organic life, such as birth and decay. History consists primarily of events, of anomalous, surprising acts and achievements that distinguish one human from another and ultimately usher in a new paradigmatic manner of living. The heroic race traitor betrays a disputatious, hand-me-down racial identity that is divisive and self-destructive to pursue a higher, austere morality that secures his esteem and allows him to view a world without dust to clearly see the manifest souls and human identities behind the fabrications of race.

The virtuous transracial cosmopolitans have no historical or biological racial identity. Rather, they are orphans forged in the vectors of their own moral imagination and an exalted vision of life's most reverent possibilities that will give rise to a tumultuous and binding moral revolution of the soul.

They have given birth to themselves and have chosen to be born. The accidents of birth—bloodline, parents, and family—are journalistic minutiae. They are incidentals of history and largely irrelevant in the face of what lies ahead—the future and the attendant emergence of moral beings. This radically autonomous, sovereign, and self-transcendent being lacks biological or historical identity. Parents are sociological details. To lose the entirety of one's ancestry is not a tragedy, but a necessary forgetting of where one came from in order to authentically create oneself anew—to genuinely be the author of one's identity.

The virtuous transracial race traitors have renounced heirship, legacy, and racial heritage. They never chose them, and since they were bequeathed to them without their permission, they cannot lay claim to a love of them, for they cannot love anything that they never consciously chose. That which was foisted upon them—race, ethnicity, national identity, and religion—have to be appraised and evaluated against the backdrop of their emergent value schema. Around their own kind, they feel boredom and the soul-killing sense of a deadening, ubiquitous, sycophantic, haunting monotony. Monotony deadens sensory perception, and they know that sensory deprivation makes them immune to the acquisition of values, and of the burgeoning, innovative drive that lies in their own soul—to the creation of a new way and of the establishment of their enterprises as the paradigmatic foundation upon which a new, emergent being can come into existence. If they could annihilate "their own kind" they would, along with their superstitious customs, traditions, mores, and protocols that are believed to function as the foundational bedrock of culture and society. If they hear the terms "social cohesion" and "civic trust" in relation to racial pride and unity once more, they will inflict a joyful cruelty on those who utter such conceptual inanities.

Only when identity is beyond blood will they see the unfolding of a new creation.

This boredom of the soul that they feel around those of their own kind causes them no shortage of existential angst and loneliness.

They have no ancestors—they recognize none who lay claim to them, for they are the tribal property of no person and would weep no more for the demise of their blood-kind as they would for a stranger who shares their values, vision, and crusade for a moral future. They have no offspring, except those with whom they have made an ethical alliance to shape a new universe, and those who, like the fourth angel, will pour their vials upon the sun and scorch men with a life-giving fire. They do not worship the family, the tribe, the race, the state, or the nation. They hold no higher value than the naked, tribally unadorned self that presents itself to them in its indubitable singularity.

Some may say theirs is a highly evacuated self that is devoid of its historicity. But they invert the dictum: "You can't know where you are heading unless you know your history," with their own mantra: "You can't arrive at the place you are creating unless you forget your history." The world, they believe, is dying from an orgy of overly historicized personalities that exist on a temporal continuum. They want to annihilate the continuum and begin the historical record anew. Their story starts with a new being—a post-human being that has transcended the constraints of blood, race, and ethnicity. They want to infuse the modern imagination with possibilities dismissed as evacuations of the soul—imprac-tical and psychologically untenable.

The virtuous cosmopolitan race traitors have, from the time they remembered themselves, regarded racial identity as anachronistic.

They want to empty history and wring it of the bloodiness of its ghastly murders, executed under the aegis of tribalism. Humanity looks to them like withered white orchids on purple branches. Rigor mortis forecloses any resurrection; a stiffened history has congealed into an indisputable record that is beyond misinterpretation—there is blood everywhere. Only when iden-tity is beyond blood will they see the unfolding of a new creation.

As hard as they tried, they had never been able (nor were they ever truly interested) in subjecting history—their own or others'—to critical scrutiny and reinterpretation. They knew that behind that enterprise lay a distortion of reality based on the premise that one is the product of one's environment. They had rejected that bromide uttered like a metaphysical absolute or law of nature with cool disregard and simply adduced themselves as evidence of its utter falsity. They had shown that some burning vision and relentless drive had inspired them to make themselves superior to circumstance. They aspired to transcend the vicissitudes and opacities of those phenomena that populate the social landscape of epochs past and present, those subtle and socially sanctioned mores by which human beings are categorized, promoted, and demoted, according to the prestige of the tribal identity the mores shore up.

They see a jarring ubiquity in all the tribal squabbles—the greatest ecological disaster of all times. Trivia, personal angst about tribal identity, and assumed superiority in the pride one feels in being a member of a superior people are elevated to the level of "brute facts."

For the moral cosmopolitan race traitor, the contretemps of tribalism and the harm they do are proper studies for the field of science. The lowest denominator to which people can sink—holding strong tribal identities and upholding the psychotic framework that sustains them—has been elevated to a status that makes it worthy of metaphysical speculation. They mourn this state of affairs and use their creative agency to refashion a new existence.

To be bound down by the soul-killing minutiae of history is an affront to the dignity of truly free individuals and their self-transcending and self-surpassing aspirational nature. Race, ethnicity, their authenticating protocols were balls and chains on their shoulders. They had wanted to fly, but not away from anything in particular, for they never granted the minutiae the significance it cried out for; rather, they wanted to fly to some future of their own—a place of regeneration and rebirth where they could conjoin themselves in a beautiful and well-earned love with others. They had thought that racial identity had expelled others from the pantheon of the community. They had felt righteous indignation and moral anger at the expurgators. Now, they realized that it was they who had never earned the proper title of human being, that it was they who had never belonged anywhere and had sought in the name of blood to uproot those who had found a home somewhere here on earth.

And what is to become of the scorched men and women and the scorched earth of those who breathe the fire of life? They, and post-human virtuous race traitors, will deracinate the *raciated* effigies who parade as ethnics and walking, balkanized automatons. In their world, race has been eradicated and abolished, and those who cling to it in psychic infantilism eventually atrophy and die from natural extinction.

If others use the term "cosmopolitan" as a coinage designating indiscriminate love of humanity and world citizenship, then the virtuous race traitors have become reactionary and moral revisionists. For theirs is a normative love. They are congenitally and institutionally incapable of loving the world and its mediocre representatives unconditionally, causelessly, and irrationally. To love mankind indiscriminately is to love a compound noun. Their love is an inspiring one, predicated on a theme of moral ambitiousness and optimistic perfection. They, the free individuals, love humanity as it might be and ought to be, not as it is—mired in the shallow present, its denizens suffering from a paucity of imagination and bereft of the capacity for continued becoming.

Their love is a command to rise to a glorious height that humankind has never imagined and failed to believe is realizable—the post-racial and post-ethnic world. The command to rise is embedded in the timorous decorum of tribal low-culture; in the soulless, demotic camps of the tribal animal with his snout to the ground, sniffing for ancestral traces to lift him in this world and give him a sense of belonging and historical anchorage in a clannish universe. The same tribal, primordial primitivism drives him deeper to sniff out the odor of ethnic and racial authenticity in every passerby—like some porcine forager—who suggests himself as a plausible candidate in a world where blood and belonging are believed to insulate one from death.

In the evolving world of porous borders, increasing immigration, and fluid social identities, those who will not grow to accommodate the spaces in which human beings matriculate will simply devolve and eventually die off. As they reach back into the atavistic registers of their being for some primordial, phylogenetic, ancestral domain that connects them with their kith and kin and blood-kind, they will descend into an abysmal void. The domain was never there; it was, instead, the product of mythological narratives that they created to eke out a false prestige from race, ethnicity, and the valorized, local spaces in which they were born. They were unable to place themselves in all possible places and in just one possible world—this earth. Their range of vision was unable to extend beyond the false prestige manufactured to demonize others and glorify and elevate them in their rottenness, their mediocrity, and their paltry attempts to wring social and ethical prestige from their morally arbitrary and neutral ethnic, racial, regional identities.

Therefore, witnessing the comic-tragic spectacle of people attempting to ride on the social and moral prestige of identities that never had and can never have a moral dimension to them, the virtuous cosmopolitan race traitors ethically mandate racial self-cleansing. Smiling like the Buddha after witnessing the grotesqueries, the charnel houses, and other houses of horror that masquerade as natural features of human identification, the virtuous cosmopolitan race traitors, in a spirit of compassion and contempt, foist a new philosophy upon the suffocating human race. Benevolent iconoclasts, they undermine the spirit of seriousness that undergirds the tribalist's schema for the world. The recurring motifs are tedious, boring, and conventional—cracker-barrel folk wisdom passed on by so-called wise elders that are nothing more than sentimental bromides, pseudo-incantations, and rhetorical plinths, recast and dressed up in a contemporary idiom of racial and ethnic solidarity, cultural authenticity, and respectful multiculturalism. It is all a contemporary repertory of conceptual inanities and orgiastic self-oblation legitimized by appeals to tradition and history and the historical record that is invoked from time to time like moral axioms.

The virtuous cosmopolitan race traitor believes, like Charles Dickens, that the relief of human misery lies not in social revolution but in a transformation of the individual heart. The first transformative move is simply an initial iteration among several to follow. It is a propitious gesture meant to ameliorate—if not abolish—the internecine warfare of tribalism.

Such a race traitor has never had the capacity to understand the pull of blood and of unchosen values in general. The attachment to ethnic/racial kinship and blood relations has always seemed like a form of delayed weaning from a protracted parental relationship. Thinking about it, the race traitor realizes that this attachment is shrouded in a blanket of unresolved familial conflicts transferred unto the *Volk*, the race, and the ethnos.

Behind that pull is the demand for unconditional love, a love that does not have to be earned and maintained but is derived from mere membership in a bloody pool of ancestral relations. He has always loved the aspirational impulse in others—those on the road to becoming by meaningful engagements with others and a process of sacred social intercourse with the best among the species. He thought that only infants could legitimately demand unconditional love and that the demand in adults was nothing more than a neurotic cry for them to remain rooted in their rottenness, a desire never to venture outside their own solipsistic confines and perspectival situatedness.

The virtuous race traitor has never been able to, in reason, understand the automatic "knowing" of others allegedly drawn from his kind. Throughout his life, he has been unable to comprehend the racial knowledge that comes from membership in a tribe. Until he has been perceived correctly and has perceived others through observation, experience, and intimacy, he has never known what it means to simply "get" one of his own. Receptive to all—the foreign and the familiar alike—the virtuous cosmopolitan has no special epistemological kinship with kith or kin, for they are as strange and as alien to him as are those from whom he is separated by language, religion, race, ethnicity, and nationality. He is, indubitably, *sui generis* and unalterably individuated. Such associations shall come from value affinities with those whom he has chosen, regardless of their tribal status.

He incurs no special obligations or loyalties to those who lay claim to his efforts by means of his membership in their tribe or clan. In having no biology, no ancestors, no parents, and no kin, and in always maintaining a tenuous and provisional relationship to his descendants and ancestors, he removes himself from the lingering haunts of memory and nostalgia; only the latter is not quite correct. He is never sentimentally nostalgic for an irretrievable golden era—unless it is universal in nature and grounded in a common human identity. He is nostalgic in another way, and he does mourn the fate of a future he will usher in by means of his own post-human humanity. He is nostalgic for a future that has not yet come—a prognostic and yet-to-be-born future whose death he foresees before it has yet to arrive. He wants to belong but cannot because his home and his kind of world have yet to be created.

With a past that has been obliterated and forgotten and a future that may arrive after his death, the virtuous cosmopolitan lives both agonistically and hopefully. Living in a habitual state of expectancy leaves him vigilant, creative, and susceptible to remissions into states of metaphysical blues. Each day, the world perishes more and more in a miasmic orgy of tribal mores applied to daily living. Each day, thousands die for no other reason than for the color of their skin, their ethnicity, and lineage. Their deaths ought to dispel the lies centered on raciated bodies that rot, smell, and disintegrate in the same ways, regardless of tribal status.

Mostly though, he takes existential alienation as an inevitable consequence of living and creating outside the botched configurations that demarcate borders and regions, countries, and states. This existential alienation is inevitable in one who has seen farther than others, dreamed longer than others, and spends more time than most in actively using his humanity to usher in the change his soul aspires to formulate. He ideates, and then he creates. He dreams, and then he fulfills those dreams. But in all his subcutaneous modes of transcendence of this world he has left behind, he is forced to live in *this* world—the one he has psychologically departed from. The alienation is not metaphysical;

it is not to be treated like an invariant law of nature. He can and will use his agency and uncompromising efforts to usher in a new kind of universe. The worlds of the tribes are lived under collective psychosis and granted legitimacy by the imprimatur of all the self-appointed officiates who function as vanguards and sentinels of more than culture or society, and of nations and states. They have assumed the temerity of stylizing lives for people under the holy rubric of the tribes and its cognate phenomena—race and ethnicity. They have mythologized what they term is the essence of human beings and spawned a narrative that anchored it within the matrices of tribal logos—the *sui generis*, indubitable, irrevocable insignia of racial authenticity. They have waged wars, perverted science, and fabricated so-called biological markers that locate racial differences among the one species that contains many different character types but that are all subsumable under the compound noun—man.

His becoming and transcendence are infinite in their capacity to take him to increasingly new levels of growth and evolution, but they are not set against his nature. Hence his alienation is not permanent because the universe is not and cannot be against the efforts he executes to simply get reality right. He knows human beings will continue to perish from the orgy of tribalism, like animals who have never lifted their snouts beyond the foot of a tree to behold the sky above and envision a new world and a new way of living.

But the virtuous race traitor is never alienated from his values and the knowledge obtained from his observations and perceptions of the world. They correspond to an objective reality that cannot be twisted like a piece of putty to fit any private evasions, public omissions, or any culturally-sanctioned perversions committed against one's fellow man in the name of some higher good such as race, the tribe, the ethnos, and the nation, to which one must sacrifice one's life and one's authentic truth.

Self-inflicted psychosis can only be maintained by two means. First, the sanction of those who spare one the consequences of living a lie and executing distortions in the world—we shall call such persons the moral enablers. Second, by the strategic manner in which those who perform as willed psychotics navigate among the registers of convenient lucidity and self-indulgent fantasy, buoyed up by the same gestures of the other game players. They act as if the fictive tropes of race and ethnicity do designate something substantially real about others (characterologically speaking), only to the extent when compelling evidence to the contrary makes them conceptual revisionists. Failure to become such will jeopardize some goal, project, experience they are forced to pursue, embark on, or hold respectively. Shifting their cognitive gears to meet the challenges of the sensory deprivation tanks they inhabit, they adhere to the dictates of reality intermittently, just long enough to gain the oxygen needed to live in the real world—the world that exists beyond markers of the tribes.

For the virtuous cosmopolitan race traitor, those who have created such markers are rapists. Tribal markers are tools of rape because they invade the humanity of persons with fictive and ultimately dehumanizing narratives.

No race or group of persons has ever been uplifted by having others label them as racial types!

The post-humanist sees the dignitarian assault waged against human well-being by racialists. They have systemically and systematically eviscerated people of their dignity and experiential identities; they have "othered" broad swaths of humanity and disambiguated them from the complex psychic infrastructures that make them complex human beings.

Tribal markers nationalize the souls of human beings by the sheer force of the ubiquity and totalizing narratives that reduce all members of a tribe to a one-size-fits-all metric of appraisal. Regardless of your evolutionary experiences in the world, in spite of how they manifest themselves within your lives, no matter how your growth has changed who you are and migrated you beyond the party lines of tribal rhetoric, regardless of how you may have disregarded the faltering bromides, clichés, incantations, and platitudes that inform the sensibilities of tribal members and give their governing narratives legitimacy—your indubitable nature as an individual is rapaciously deprivatized. It is robbed of its luminous singularity. Imposed on it is a generic agency, devised from a one-size-fits-all script that is the repository of stereotypes, caricatures, and untold myths that purport to predict your future actions, interpret your past, and deny you the full reality of your present experience. This script authenticates you by virtue of how closely you adhere to the consensus among its adherents, whose numeric preponderance constitutes evidence of the truth or falsity of your behavior and actions vis-à-vis the sacred script *they* have devised.

The script robs you of your glory and democratizes it by appropriating your achievements and turning them into collective tribal property. It belongs to them because you belong to them; you are one of them—their kind. The psychic sequestration of the individual by the tribe not only leaves him evacuated of his attributes and the radical freedom to interpret them and accord them value significance in his life as he sees fit. He is left bereft of the capacity to jettison the interpretation and judgments others have rendered against his life. The generic agency he is assumed to hold becomes normalized as invariant laws of nature. He becomes an overdetermined automaton who is expected to live in the make-believe world of the tribalist. When his generic agency becomes codified in the minds of others as an unassailable social fact, reappraisal, modification, and revision of the systems of identity and value that accrue to his agency become daunting feats of courage. Having the courage to exercise one's humanity against the backdrop of all human types outside the tribe and embrace and celebrate the expansion of identity that results from a fearless and appetitive self-inclusion in the nuclear lives of others—strangers, foreigners, and all those outside his kith and kin—becomes a demanding endeavor.

Seeking to enter the world of others without the protective barriers of tribal prestige, or with an ethnic and/or racial interface to broker such encounters, the cosmopolitan race traitor sheds the old skin of his past lives and rapturously lives a life in the present with the varied and complex experiential, personality, and value accoutrements of the so-called radical others to inspire him. He lives beyond and outside the tribal narratives that regulate the moral, personal, and existential lives of others. By this means, he knows he can truly love humanity. He knows that individual agency is a restoration of privacy and glory back to the individual where it properly belongs.

His post-humanity entails living beyond the outdated markers that have constituted a politics of identity. It is the insignia for a new planetary ethos and ethics. This model of living cannot be manifested by living on the peripheries or the margins. He cannot live as a decentralized subject, for that would make him an outsider to a world he aspires to inhabit. His post-humanity positions him in a new realm in which life beyond the historical accoutrements of race and tribal markers have ceased to exist. The world that fetishizes such markers and grants them their moral and metaphysical potency has shrunk largely because psychosis, when protracted and when it undergirds a life, eventually becomes monotonous. Monotony leads to sensory deprivation as it deadens imagination, creative drive, and perception. Obstructed perception deeply compromises how one navigates oneself in the world. To perceive reality incorrectly is to risk psychological and physical injury and even death.

In this new space, the assumed correlates among skin pigmentation, ethnicity, and moral agency have disappeared beyond respectable debate. Again, he adduces himself as evidence of the irrelevancy of respectable conversations about tribal markers. He has peeled himself down to a thin core, abstracted from all the meaningful moments in his life—those that filled his body with vitality and his soul with exuberance were racially and ethnically irrelevant. Given his sensibilities, he could have supplanted them anywhere on earth and retained the spontaneity and vitality that are his bodily trademarks.

This is because the development of a transracial ethos can be a symbiotic two-pronged project, engaging in dialogue with its historical architects and allowing the dialogue and the attendant refinement of one's ethical sensibilities to organically unfold in the world where human beings meet and live. To hold this position, while convincing individuals that a transracial cosmopolitan is not a lifestyle that only educated privileged people can embrace, is to play one more role in the division of labor on behalf of his life. The task is to find ways to socialize nonintellectuals by means of his universal cosmopolitan virtues and values. This is not just the creation of morality. It is also something of a dance—an interaction among strangers where the rules of engagement are intuited by signals accessed in the moment and where each step is determined by the reciprocity of exchanges.

Cosmopolitan virtues of this type are born from an attitude where radical intersubjectivity is neither abhorred nor embraced as a form of exoticism or patronization—the latter dehumanizes. Rather, radical intersubjectivity is freedom to be deeply touched by another and allow spontaneous gestures and responses that blossom from the encounter to shape a new identity. It might resist the terminologies and labels of the social world. Still, it corresponds to the psychological and moral terrain of one's inner life. This is the gift-giving feature of humanity precisely in our control and need not depend on the political machinery of the state or other institutions that effect changes in our social lives. I would refer to this cosmopolitan virtue as the art of *moral genuflection*. Protracted genuflection—as a way of life—would be a form of radical intersubjectivity. For the sake of simplicity, I'll refer to it as the willingness to grant oneself permission to be deeply penetrated by the humanity of another person, where that humanity can call into question the very core of one's social identity and where it forces one to make that identity negotiable. It is the willingness to hand over your continued socialization to others (good judgments prevailing, of course; we're not talking about serial killers and rapists). It means that we see socialization as an ongoing process that does not stop at legal adulthood. It is a humbling and gift-giving aspect of human living. We help each other shape a new identity or transform an ongoing one in a rigorous and morally enduring manner. This is the gift-giving feature of our humanity that we own and the deepest source of love we can offer those we call strangers. It is one way of making the world more lovable in a two-fold manner—first, as value-makers and valuers who love in the world and thereby make the world more lovable, and second, by loving in the world because there is much that is lovable and ought to be loved.

This two-fold manner of loving is another way of also achieving and practicing creative moral agency simultaneously. Radical intersubjectivity is not passive submission, neither is it a form of inactive spectatorship. This gift-giving feature of our humanity—anathema to the spirit of every variant of tribalism, whether it takes the form of cultural nationalism or racial particularity—is the humble capacity to genuflect before the other in a spirit of reciprocity and respectful brotherhood and sisterhood and say: "I am not so complete that I can resist handing you some part of my continued socialization and identity formation as a human being. With you, my friend, my humanity—regardless of its origins—continues to expand and will take me to places I could never have imagined."

I regard this gift-giving impulse as part of how we organically make cosmopolitan values as human beings. One says further in the genuflection: "We share a common humanity, and in that sacred space, something of the Divine is achieved. I open myself as a canvas on which you may inscribe your wisdom, teachings, and generosity—or whatever seeds of it you may have discovered in your own soul."

This is the gift-giving nature of the virtuous cosmopolitan race traitor who disarms the racialist and grants, to those struggling to get beyond the soul-killing narratives of its ubiquitous racial scripts, a patina of hope that a life beyond psychological race is possible.

I am not and never have been interested in relating to human beings as ethnics, races, or even national constructs. I am profoundly in love with this world of mine. When I see a person who does not speak the same language as I do, whose ethnic and national origins are different from mine, I look in her eyes. A smile appears on her face, and I, too, smile because any gesture of the beautiful in the human is infectious. I smile. I am at peace, and all bewildering thoughts about how it is possible that people can feel love only for their "own kind" dissipate. We share a smile, and I know that we share a humanity.

Transracial moral cosmopolitans are individuals who, against their origins, choose a nonracial identity. They have psychically transcended the primordial muck of race. They recognize that human identity is made and lived; it is not a "natural" feature of the world. Moreover, the transracial cosmopolitan identity is a weaned identity. Unlike the childlike creatures of their surroundings who cling to ethnic and racial identities the way a neurotic forty-year-old clings to his mother's skirt, moral cosmopolitans have no preference for their "own kind."

There are those, undoubtedly, who will argue that my viewpoint is naïve, unrealistic, and impractical. To hold a nonracial identity is to be removed from a deep sense of who a person makes him or herself to be. Morality is, however, a very demanding enterprise. Its function is not to mirror what we necessarily desire on the spur of the moment. Unlike friends, who we sometimes chose as clones of ourselves, morality cannot reproduce the images we wish to create to assuage the fears and insecurities of modern life. Moral living is an act of faith. We leap and know that we will be radically redefined by a process whose endpoint we cannot conceptually fathom but whose instructional guidance is necessary for our very survival. No moral system can entreat its students to aspire to the best and highest form of living if it does not demand much of them. Psychological realism does not require that we water down our moral systems to fit the conception of human nature in fashion at the moment. The moral self cannot be twisted like putty to fit the mutating perversions of a modern culture that beguiles its inhabitants with cosmetic appearances of their souls and inculcates in them the idea that their essence is to be found in their racial identities. Psychological realism demands that any moral system assume a set of basic attributes about the human person that can be practiced because it is humanly possible. Moral cosmopolitanism, then, is concerned not so much with the conception of self-persons find themselves valorizing but, instead, with the future self, the *not-yet self*—the self that ought to exist. Morality, above all, is the journey of moral becoming and retransformation.

The future is theirs because, out of their broken pasts and souls, they looked up and saw a vision, not just of life's better possibilities, but the other half of themselves that had been left uncultivated, uncorrupted, and untouched. Step by step they created a future that was theirs to mold. Hesitantly, yet confidently, and often with great trepidation, they took possession of an American world they were told they could never belong to.

Equally vital to the vision of the virtuous cosmopolitan race traitor is the act of radical forgiveness. Those whose lives might have been marred by, for example, the ravages of racial discrimination of Jim Crow segregationist laws, live far richer spiritual lives by practicing radical forgiveness towards those who oppressed them than they would by seeking retributive justice. This is because an obsession with justice and entitlement shackles the soul to the compensations of the one who has harmed one. A spirit of aggrievement, paradoxically, places one in a dependent role on the other, One is not free. Radical forgiveness frees the soul from resentment and fosters an ethic of care towards those who have harmed one. It not only forges radically new relationships, but it also heralds a model for a new type of humanity, a new planetary ethic and humanism devoid of bitterness.

Free and living in that space of radical love and forgiveness, the virtuous man or woman, holding no racial identity as his standard-bearer, stands confidently with palms facing the universe and declares to the world, "I have no history. I have no race. I have only you, and the future."

REFERENCES

Introduction

Coates, Ta-Nehisi, *We Were Eight Years in Power.* New York: One World, 2017.

Woodson, Robert L. Sr., *Lessons From The Least of These: The Woodson Principles.* New York: Bombardier Books, 2020.

Chapter One

Eze, Emanuel, *Achieving Our Humanity: The Idea of the Postracial Future.* New York: Routledge, 2001.

Hegel, Georg Wilhelm Friedrich, *Lectures on the Philosophy of World History.* Cambridge, Mass: Cambridge University Press, 1976.

Paglia, Camille, *Sexual Personae: Art and Decadence from Nefertiti to Emily Dickinson.* New Haven, CT: Yale University Press, 1990.

Senghor, Leopold S., "Psychology of the African Negro," in *African Philosophy: Selected Readings*. Edited by Albert G. Mosely. Englewood Cliffs, NJ: Prentice Hall, 1995.

Wiredu, Kwasi, "How Not to Compare African Thought with Western Thought," in *African Philosophy: Selected Readings*. Edited by Albert G. Mosely. Englewood Cliffs, NJ: Prentice Hall, 1995.

CHAPTER TWO

Douglass, Frederick, *Great Speeches by Frederick Douglass*. New York: Dover Publications, 2013.

D'Souza, Dinesh, *What's So Great About America*. New York: Regnery Publishing, 2015.

Encyclopaedia Britannica, *The Founding Fathers: The Essential Guide to the Men Who Made America*. Wiley, 2007.

Jefferson, Thomas, *The Portable Thomas Jefferson*. Edited by Merrill D. Peterson. New York: Penguin Books, 1975.

Lincoln, Abraham, *Collected Works of Lincoln, Vol. 2*. Rutgers, NJ: Rutgers University Press, 1953.

Rand, Ayn, *The Romantic Manifesto: A Philosophy of Literature*. New York: Signet; 2nd Revised Edition, 1971.

Thompson, C. Bradley, *America's Revolutionary Mind: A Moral History of the American Revolution and the Declaration that Defined It.* New York: Encounter Books, 2019.

CHAPTER THREE

Brook, Yaron and Watkins, Don, *Equal Is Unfair: America's Misguided Fight Against Income Inequality.* New York: St. Martin's Press, 2016.

Du Bois, W.E.B., *The Souls of Black Folk.* New York: Penguin, 2002.

Rand, Ayn, *The Ayn Rand Lexicon: Objectivism from A to Z.* Edited by Harry Binswanger. New York: New American Library, 1988.

"War on Poverty." Wikipedia. Wikimedia Foundation, April 28, 2021. https://en.wikipedia.org/wiki/War_on_poverty.

CHAPTER FOUR

Bawer, Bruce, *The Victims' Revolution: The Rise of Identity Studies and the Closing of the Liberal Mind.* New York: HarperCollins, 2012.

DiAngelo, Robin, *White Fragility: Why It's So Hard for White People to Talk About Racism.* Boston: Beacon Press, 2018.

Gordon, Jane Anna and Gordon, Lewis ed., *A Companion to African-American Studies.* Hoboken, NJ: Wiley-Blackwell, 2006.

Kendi, Ibram X., *How to Be an Antiracist*. New York: One World, 2019.

Peikoff, Leonard, *The Ominous Parallels: The End of Freedom in America*. New York: Plume, 1983.

Riley, Jason, *Please Stop Helping Us: How Liberals Make It Harder for Blacks to Succeed*. New York: Encounter Books, 2014.

Steele, Shelby, *White Guilt: How Blacks and Whites Together Destroyed the Promise of The Civil Rights Era*. New York: HarperCollins, 2006.

Warren, Calvin, "Black Nihilism and the Politics of Hope" *The New Centennial Review*, Vol. 15 No. 1, 2015, pp. 215-248.

Wilderson, Frank B. III, *Afropessimism*. New York: Liveright, 2020.

CHAPTER FIVE

Derek, Heater, *World Citizenship and Government: Cosmopolitan Ideas in the History of Western Political Thought*. New York: St. Martin's Press, 1996.

Heschel, Abraham, *Who is Man?* Stanford, CA: Stanford University Press, 1965.

Hill, Jason, *Becoming a Cosmopolitan: What it Means to Be a Human Being in the New Millennium*. Lanham, MD: Rowman & Littlefield, 2011.

Hill, Jason, *Beyond Blood Identities: Posthumanity in the Twenty-First Century*. Lanham, MD: Lexington Books, 2009.

Jaspers, Karl, *Way to Wisdom: An Introduction to Philosophy*. Eastford, CT: Martino Fine Books, 2015.

Rand, Ayn, "Racism" in *The Virtue of Selfishness: A New Concept of Egoism*. New York: Signet, 1964.

Waters, Mary C., *Ethnic Options: Choosing Identities in America*. Berkeley, CA: University of California Press, 1990.

West, Cornel, *Race Matters*. New York: Vintage Reprints, 1994.

Zack, Naomi, *Philosophy of Science and Race*. New York: Routledge, 2002.

ACKNOWLEDGMENTS

This book would not have been possible without the immediate response of my publisher and editor, David Bernstein, who became convinced that it was worth publishing immediately after I pitched the idea to him. He remains the best editor I have been blessed to have in the writing and publishing of five books.

My thanks to my editors at *FrontPage Magazine*, especially to Jamie Glazov, and to David Horowitz, CEO and owner of the Freedom Center, for permitting me to publish several of the ideas contained in this book in my column. Mark Tapson has treated my columns with care.

My copyeditor, Michelle Nati, who is perfection personified, has made me a better writer.

The support of particular friends during the intense months of the writing of this book comes to mind. They are Beth Feeley, Mary Amico, Mike Shereck, Sarah Stern, Jon Sutz, Charles Negy, Richard Becker. I thank Ryne Degrave for close friendship and deep interest in my ideas. Richard Engle is a dear friend and keen interlocutor who challenges my thinking. Thanks to T. Nevada Powe for forty-five years of steady friendship and profound intellectual engagement, and my Facebook community who, believe it or not, have become daily correspondents.

New friends inspire me to carry on with new projects. They are, Niall Ferguson, Ayaan Hirsi Ali, John Greig, Peter Boghossian, and Greg Ellis.

Dr. Bob Shillman is always there to encourage my warrior spirit and support me in all my endeavors. I am especially grateful to my mother, who never has to always agree with my ideas to give her support of my work and affirmation of my existence.